Also by the same author

'they did; you can' (Crown House 2008)
'Ten Steps To Excellence' (Talbot 2008)
'inspired' (Talbot 2009)

Impossible to Inevitable

The Catalyst for Positive Change

Michael Finnigan

authorHOUSE®

AuthorHouse™ UK Ltd.
500 Avebury Boulevard
Central Milton Keynes, MK9 2BE
www.authorhouse.co.uk
Phone: 08001974150

First published in 2003

1ˢᵗ reprint 2005

2ⁿᵈ reprint 2006

Published by AuthorHouse 5/26/2010

ISBN: 978-1-4490-4426-8 (sc)

Library of Congress Control Number: 2009912330

Revised and re-edited by Michael Finnigan and Andrew O'Donoghue 2009

First printed in Great Britain by The Charlesworth Group, Wakefield
First published by Talbot Publications: j.talbot@virgin.net

All illustrations copyright© Lucy Finnigan

This book is printed on acid-free paper.

"All men dream: but not equally.
Those who dream by night in the dusty
recesses of their minds wake in the day
to find that it was vanity: but the dreamers
of the day are dangerous men, for they may
act their dreams with open eyes, to make it possible."

T.E. Lawrence,
The Seven Pillars of Wisdom

At the dawn of the second Millennium, the scale, speed and brutality of the forces unleashed into the world stripped away the collective global breath.

Ignorance and complacency of the need to change and adapt were swept aside, leaving in their place an immense vacuum, populated only with the words, 'but how?'

Even America's erstwhile biggest and most favourite business, General Motors, was brought savagely to its knees to humbly and in total desperation seek protection from bankruptcy via the safe haven of US Law.

Whilst the survival strategies and battle plans are desperately debated and drawn up in Boardrooms across the world, the battle grounds remain the factories, offices, shops, and homes which continue to be the embattled front lines of vital service delivery.

i2i exists to equip your people, at all levels, with the skills and motivation to transform your organisations in response to the world's challenge of change, passionately and positively; to enable them to both lead and take part in that change, enthusiastically and energetically; inspirationally and infectiously.

We live in unprecedented times.

This book contains uplifting examples of extraordinary people who are thriving in them.

Contents

INTRODUCTION

by Michael Finnigan & Andrew O'Donoghue

When we first got together to form a company to help people in all walks of life; to help businesses and organisations of all types transform the results they achieve, by learning to change the way they think, we set mighty goals. We dreamed bold, magnificent and audacious dreams.

Some would have said that our goals and dreams were impossible (and some actually did...to our faces!)

Who would have thought, back in 1996, that by now we would be honoured to have worked with Fire Fighters, Doctors, Policemen and Policewomen, Teachers, an International Soccer Team, International Cricket Teams, a championship winning Rugby Team, European Tour Championship and Ryder Cup Winning Golfers, a Formula One Racing Team, World Cup Winning and Champions League Winning Soccer Players, and a Champion Ice Skater?

Who would have dreamed that we would help get a football team to Wembley and then to win at the Millennium Stadium in Cardiff, that we would be in the 'dugout' at Manchester United, Liverpool, Arsenal and Chelsea, pitting our wits against the likes of Wenger, Benitez, José Mourinho and the great Sir Alex Ferguson himself, against other World Cup Winners, and against Michael Owen, David Beckham, Fernando Torres, Cristiano Ronaldo, Ryan Giggs, and Wayne Rooney?

Who would have imagined back then the **world's biggest businesses and best known brands** as our clients?

Who would believe we would address one single audience of 28,000 people or work with people from Mexico, China, the USA, Sri Lanka, Australia, Scandinavia, the Baltics, and, of course, the UK and Europe?

Our clients serve millions of customers every day, non-stop, advertise on television hundreds of times every day all over the world, and are responsible for hundreds of thousands of jobs!

Who would have dared to imagine that we would feature on national television and radio, in national newspapers and magazines, and even in the odd best-selling autobiography?

A man once said 'what the mind can conceive and believe, the mind can achieve'.

Well, he was right! We really do feel so lucky to be living our dreams.

The title of this book says it all really – what may at first seem *'impossible'*, can, with desire and belief become *'inevitable'*.

This book is full of amazing stories of ordinary, yet extraordinary people.

We could have chosen to write about ourselves, but that can wait for a long time! We could have written about those 'rich and famous' clients we have just mentioned, of which there are many. We could have spouted our philosophy of success and happiness. But all that has been done, hasn't it?

Then it occurred to us that what we really had here was an opportunity to honour those who had made the journey, who had listened to the principles we showed them, and had used the tools they had acquired with outstanding results.

So then it came to seeking out the 'Anonymous Achievers', and convincing them to tell their stories. This was easier than anticipated; people were happy to tell their stories, and did so with modesty and gritty, realistic eloquence. It was obvious even then, that their words must live on the page, and so the format was decided.

These people tell their stories through unrehearsed dialogues, and the spontaneity of the interviews is captured for you to enjoy. Sometimes, they will refer to '**the course**', and will use terms they learned from and associate with it. If you know what they mean, or if you needed to be reminded, terrific. If you do not know what they mean, that should not detract from the story, though if it does, visit us on the web at **www.i2i-121.com** and find out when the next 'course' place is available.

Our hope is that at least one of the stories will touch you deeply, making you realise that your battle has been fought before, and with success.

Bob Champion, the legendary winner of The Grand National Steeple Chase in 1981 on Aldaniti, equally famous for his successful battle against cancer, said, when interviewed on the BBC by David Coleman, immediately after the race:

'I HOPE MY WINNING SHOWS PEOPLE THAT THERE IS ALWAYS HOPE AND THAT

ALL BATTLES CAN BE WON'

We know that he is right. All battles can be won, and the heroic people in our book prove it. Everyone interviewed here is happy and successful, undoubtedly top performers in their field, yet the point is that it wasn't always that way for them, and the one thing they share in common with each other, is that they were taught principles by us which provided the catalyst they needed to make the changes they went on to make.

These people made the journey. Mike was first introduced to the concept of needing to think positively in 1986 by Bernard Walsh, an entrepreneur who told him that reading *'Think and Grow Rich'* by Napoleon Hill had first changed and then saved his life. Bernard told him many years later that by lending him the book, he was trying to help 'an ambitious young man', but the message went way over Mike's head at the time; he was obviously just not ready.

It wasn't until he met Art Niemann, in November of 1992, that he saw his first glimpse of a world that he never knew existed.

Art worked closely with the great W Clement Stone, and probably knew him better than any other man alive. Stone himself was a friend and latterly partner of Napoleon Hill. The world really is small.

Rubbing shoulders with these great men helped Mike "find (his) true path in life" and in a small way, this book is written in gratitude for their inspiration.

Art Niemann has become a good friend, business partner, and mentor, and his visits to the UK delight us all. Sadly, his influential mentor Mr Stone died on 4th September 2002, just four months into his one hundred and first year. We never met Mr Stone to thank him in person, although Mike did write a tribute for his 100th Birthday Book, which we know he enjoyed.

We dedicate this book to our families, friends and colleagues, and to Messrs Niemann and Stone, without whom none of this would have happened.

To these two great men, our eternal thanks.

Enjoy these stories of amazing human endeavour against the odds; allow them to inspire you as they, and the terrific people who achieved them, have inspired us. Please use any space provided to make notes, highlight points, underline text, and just make this book yours. Take time to do the 'Relate and Assimilate' exercises to ensure you gain maximum benefit from your reading.

So, are you, or is someone you know going to make the journey too, with i2i as your guide?
If it happens, let us know, because you, or they, might make the next book, and that is i2i's challenge to you.

Oh yes, and remember, even if something seems '*impossible*' right now, with enough desire and belief, it will simply become '*inevitable*'.

Yours Positively,

Michael Finnigan and Andrew O'Donoghue

Michael Finnigan

Third Generation

In 1980, I formed Art Niemann and Company on a shoestring. One goal was to teach the PMA concepts of W. Clement Stone to as many people as possible...young and old.

The company had a steady and quality growth as I travelled throughout North America, speaking to thousands of wonderful people.

In 1992, I got the opportunity to expand to the United Kingdom. Little did I know what a tremendous impact the trip would have on the company and myself...all because of a special and talented person...Michael Finnigan.

The training was designed to introduce the AVA concepts to Michael and other executives of a consultation company...a first for me and AVA.

On the first day of class, Michael greeted me with that million dollar smile. I knew this would be the beginning of a special and unique relationship. His interest and learning capacity amazed me as he quickly related and assimilated the many principles, always keeping that wonderful smile and enthusiasm.

He was a joy to have in the program as he became not only the top student, but the group leader as well. I offered him the opportunity to become a special student and go beyond the class. His resounding 'yes' set us on the path to a beautiful and loving relationship that has enriched both of our lives and business successes. I knew he was a winner and that he and I would form a master mind alliance to teach thousands and thousands of people throughout the world a better way to live through PMA.

Today we are still striving to make things happen and to make this a better world for this and future generations.

Michael Finnigan not only has learned and applied the PMA principles in his life, but has shared them with countless thousands as he strives to make everyday a PMA day.

What a lucky day for me and those who are fortunate to attend his programmes throughout the world.

Thanks Mike, and keep striving to achieve your greatness.

Art Niemann, Founder, Art Niemann and Company.

A message from Jimmy White
'THE WHIRLWIND FIGHTS BACK'

In February 1998, *The Sunday Times* ran an article about me, a full page story in fact, detailing my spectacular free fall, not only in terms of my snooker, but in terms of my life.

They didn't know the half of it, though my admission of addictions, mainly to gambling and alcohol, problems with my marriage to Maureen, massive bouts of depression following the deaths of my brother and mother, my bankruptcy, loss of sponsors, my battle with cancer and my split from my manager, Barry Hearn, were enough to be going on with.

No wonder I had slipped in the world snooker rankings from the pinnacle of being Number One, to a demoralising rank of 37. Snooker was almost the last thing on my mind. It was however the thing that paid the bills, and the ONLY thing that could get me out of the hole I was in.

Andrew O'Donoghue read that article and luckily for me, he was a Jimmy fan. He took the article into the office and told a disbelieving Mike that they should contact me and offer to help. Mike apparently thought that the stresses associated with starting up their business had taken their toll on Andrew, and that he'd actually 'done a Jimmy', and flipped!

Andrew was serious and wrote me a letter, addressed to me at Match Room, Barry Hearn's office. The letter finally arrived and was read to me by my daughter, Lauren. It offered to help, somehow sounded really genuine, and begged me to call if I was interested. I was as low as I'd ever been, so I called, expecting only to find that this O'Donoghue bloke was leading a team of 'Moonies' and I told him so too! He reassured me enough to get me to agree to a meeting in Esher.

I met Andrew and Mike the following week, and soon sussed out that they really weren't barmy; strange yes, but alright. We agreed that Mike would spend a couple of days with me, and I think he was even more scared than I was. After about ten minutes in our house, he was the one thinking he was stuck with the 'Moonies'. We make the Osbournes look normal, we do!

Still, talk about 'having your drains unblocked'! He sorted my head out in about the first three hours, never mind the two days; it was unbelievable! I slept solid for the first night in years. I knew then I could make it back from the brink. I felt fantastic.

When I drew the great Stephen Hendry in the World Championships, I did more work with Mike and Andrew, and just knew I was going to blow him away. I did - 10-4; my first ever victory against him in major tournament play; I even went 7-0 up, finishing the first day 8-1 up, and the snooker world thought they were dreaming!

Thanks to these boys my troubles are behind me now. I'm no angel, not perfect, and I know Mike and Andrew think I can do better. But I've got it together again, me and Maureen have our little boy and our girls, my money is sorted, I'm healthier than ever, and I did claw my way back up the rankings to that top sixteen. And I've not finished yet, believe me.

I just know I wouldn't have made it without these lads, they are the best, and I've said that to the press and the cameras many times.

If you're fighting your battle and losing, like I was, then let them help you, because they can and they will. Just give them and yourself a chance.

'Impossible to Inevitable?' Yeah, I'll buy that; I'm not in the book, but I'm one of them alright. And by the way, you could have got odds of 1000 to 1 at any bookmakers of me being 8-1 ahead in the game against Hendry!

Do I need to say anymore?

God bless.

Jimmy White

'Taxi!'

A message from Michael Whitlow, Captain, Bolton Wanderers English Premier League Soccer Team

When I heard about this book, I wanted to write a note to thank Mike and Andrew, so here goes.

The 2001–2002 football season was by far the most successful I've had on the field, and the most satisfying off it.

I'd been involved in football for fourteen years, and had been lucky enough to play in two championship winning teams with Leeds United, played in two winning play-off teams, and was a League Cup winner with Leicester City.

However, the most pleasing and proudest moment in my career was when I was voted Players' Player of the Year by my Bolton team mates, and without doubt, that comes down to the help of Mike and Andrew.

I'll always remember from our first meeting that this man Finnigan was full of energy. He made the whole room, me and my team mates, realise how one person with enthusiasm can have such an effect on those around them.

I remember this little bit more than most; he told us that we are all the 'drivers of a taxi', so we had to just 'get in and decide where you want to go'. It's like life; we have choices and can always decide which direction we take. This has stuck with me ever since.

Mike had a great effect on our team spirit, because each and every one of us wants to do their best for each other. Even the lads who are disappointed not to be playing are fully behind the others. This makes it far easier, and stops people from being selfish, and helps them take their chance in the team when it comes along.

I've learned from Mike and Andrew, not to judge others by your own ways, but to understand the different characters, and help them along in the best way possible. Some like to moan, some are 'softies' who act tough, so need an arm around them every now and again. Others need shouting at or moaning at to get them going, and so knowing your team mates on and off the field helps.

I've also learned from them not to worry about what others think of you; just be true to yourself, do the best you can, and when you come off the field, make sure you have no 'could haves', 'should haves' or 'if onlys', as you are then only doubting how hard you have pushed yourself.

Working with Mike and Andrew means setting goals, and as a team, in

2000, we wanted to survive a Premiership campaign and prove ALL the experts wrong. Most of all though, we wanted to prove to ourselves, as a team and as individuals, that we could do well in the best football league in the world.

The lads have taken on board how the brain plays such an important part in sport. If you believe in yourself and your team mates, if you trust them and help each other out on the field, it can help immensely and bring the rewards for so much hard work.

So how have they helped me personally? Well, I learned to listen to others around me and not get uptight with others if things do go wrong. I've learned to relax and for the first time in my life to sit down and enjoy reading, mainly sports related books. I believe now that I can take on the best in the world and do myself justice each time.

Mike helped me set goals and has become a true friend. I hope that he and Andrew looked at me and at Bolton Wanderers as a team and took great pride in what they achieved. The coaches, players and the Club as a whole made great strides in progressing, and that was down to the belief instilled by them.

On a personal note I have found out more about myself working with them than ever before, and what a good feeling that has been. It has not all been plain sailing, but whenever it got tough, I just thought, 'Dig deep and be true to yourself', and as I said, what a great honour to be the Players' Player of the Year.

So, thanks for all the belief and time spent working with me. I will always be grateful and will now remain positive not just for now, but for the rest of my life.

Thanks a million.

Micky Whitlow

AN ASTONISHING DEBUT

I was so astonished at watching Jimmy White demolish Stephen Hendry in the 1998 World Snooker Championships that I called the BBC Snooker Commentator, Dougie Donalie, to see if he could get the number of the 'Motivator' Jimmy had been telling everyone about.

Michael tells me I called him around 8.30 the morning after Jimmy's victory over Stephen, his first of their careers, and asked him to meet me to discuss working with some of our talented young Golfers.

We met at the BMW Championship at Wentworth a couple of weeks later and overlooking the 18th green Michael explained his approach to us.

Working with him would not be just about our approaches to our 'sport', but about our approaches to 'life', and we also learned that the whole team would be involved and not just the individuals.

It was probably more than we originally expected, but proved well worth the effort for all of us.

Everyone really enjoyed working with Mike and benefited hugely, with many recording outstanding career highlights that stand to this day.

Through Lancashire Cricket Club, Mike worked over many years with another young man in our sporting stable you might have heard of, Andrew Flintoff, who regularly tied in visits to his parents with trips to Mike's office in Preston.

I always remember Mike was the only person I'd ever met who never liked calling me 'Chubby', and I'm not now, so maybe he even won that one too!

Chubby Chandler, CEO, International Sports Management Group

Come On!

'We knew that if we were able to unlock the energy and talent within our team, we could help drive the business to new levels of performance.

What we didn't know was how to find the all elusive ingredient to make it happen....

It was then that we were introduced to Michael Finnigan, and it was the first step in what has been an incredible journey.

Over 200 senior people in our team experienced this journey at close quarters, and hundreds more in conferences across the group.

Not only has performance improved, but it changed people's attitude at work and at home.

We never looked back from that moment and the proof is in our results.

For many it has been a truly life changing experience, and as Michael and I often say to each other....come on !!'

Trevor Orman
Director, Civil Aerospace
Rolls Royce

My Mate Finn

I first met Mike Finnigan in an executive box at the Reebok Stadium at the conclusion to a thrilling Lancashire derby between Bolton Wanderers and Blackburn Rovers, my team. It was August 2003. At the time Mike was working for Sam Allardyce and Bolton Wanderers. Our emotions at that first meet could not have been more different. I was elated as my team had equalized in the last minute of the game after looking dead and buried at half time with the scores at 2-0 to the Whites.

He had a lot to say about the game, about the belief of the team and what it was that led to a seemingly unassailable lead being lost. I was struck then by his charisma and positivity. Since then we have helped each other out.

I'll give you one example. At late notice I asked him to come and join me at an Insider breakfast event on leadership in Lancashire. It was a hard event to get people out of bed for at the crack of dawn. One speaker didn't even turn up. But it was and is a really important issue. People running businesses need to be aware of their responsibilities, of their mission and how absolutely bloody brilliant it is to have that ability to turn someone's day from a good one to great one.

Finn was the star attraction. He energized the room. He didn't literally grab people by the lapels and tell them to smile, shout, scream and laugh, but he might as well have done.

One of the other panel members, a really good guy called Clive Memmott, came out of himself that day. He was running Business Link in Preston at the time and must have had one of those jobs where you can either be sucked under the quicksand with the politics or bureaucracy, or you come out fighting. I saw Clive fight that day. I truly believe Finn showed him a glimpse of what he could be if he knew he couldn't possibly fail.

And me? I'm a cynical journalist by background. Looking at the matrix of organizational roles that Finn first showed me I've probably been a terrorist in the past. I've also worked with people who are energy sappers. I won't have it any more. You have that one opportunity to make your mark. Whoever you are and whatever you do, you matter and people around you will react to how you are. When I'm old and grey and look back on these fantastic years at Insider, I'll rightly be pleased with a few different articles, the odd witty headline and some crazy design on a front cover like our smiley face in February 2009 when everyone was ready to throw themselves off one of the tall (and empty) buildings in Manchester city centre.

But the one aspect of the job that brings me the most pride is the development of the people I've been lucky enough to work with. Seeing them bloom sometimes brings a lump to my throat. They've done it all themselves because they are keen to get on. But we all help each other out and have that environment of self improvement, positivity and risk taking. If you ask them, they might have a different take on it all, but I know what I've seen. It is so important to recognize that no-one sets out to have a crap day and be rubbish. Some people might not be up to the standards we set, and they'll be happier somewhere else.

And I'm dead serious about this as well. Mike Finnigan taught me the value of positive thinking and the infectious nature of positive people. My wife Rachel is one, she has lifted my life and filled me with joy. My children have that zeal. When they are not, it is because they are hungry, or tired.

Mike Finnigan is endlessly entertaining to be around. When he left his last business to set up i2i he said he "just wanted to be great around people". What a job! What a statement. What a guy. You can be great around me anytime.

Michael Taylor, Editor, Insider Magazine

What Jeremy learned from Mike and the i2i Team

For years I shouldered the burden in our business of being 'the boss' son'. It took me a long time to learn to deal with this and drove me to want to be a success. This, perhaps as much as anything else, carried me on and led directly to the development of a business which had combined sales of £54million, was a market leader, and was perceived as a great place to work where everyone had a stake in the success of the organisation.

It was also a business that we sold in early 2009 for a sum six times higher than it had been worth eight years earlier.

Looking back you can point to great products, a very clear understanding of our customers' needs, superb customer service and a phenomenal sales operation all wrapped up in a clearly expressed strategy understood throughout the company. All the usual stuff.

But that wasn't it.......**it was all about the PEOPLE!** After all they designed the products, delivered the customer service, created the strategy and so on. Without the people businesses are just a loose collection of bricks and concrete, machinery and wire.

Putting it bluntly if you don't get the people right you'll never get the business right!

Don't get me wrong there are plenty of examples of firms who treat their staff badly and are still successful but it's my view that their success comes in spite of these attitudes and not because of them.

How much more successful could they be if they took working with their people seriously?

So is it as simple as that? Be nice to everyone and your business will thrive?

No of course not - but it has to be one of the fundamental planks upon which a business is built. It's my view that the development of the people side of a business relies on some key principles and perhaps the most important is that of understanding how people tick and for that I needed help to understand the issues.

Yes, I could sense on an intuitive level that certain behaviours on my part would tend to lead to positive responses but it was difficult to know how to harness the issues in a manner that could be formed up into a cohesive culture for the business.

As so often happens in life the answers to these questions found me rather than me finding them. By chance I met Michael Finnigan in the latter part of 1999 and we started to explore how we could develop a culture within the business designed to allow both individuals and the firm as a whole to reach its full potential.

Right at the heart of my plan was the need to understand how people tick.....why do they behave the way they do, how can we positively influence this behaviour and how can we get the best out of everyone?

I'm sure you've had experiences in your life where some noted speaker has taken what you intuitively know to be true but explained in a manner that just makes so much sense and in a way that you never could have. That's what happened with Mike – his 'i2i' Seminar brought everything into focus allowing me for the first time to clearly understand why and how you can work with people to get the best out of them.

At the heart of this for me, was the realisation that what people project is not necessarily what they really are. In other words to truly understand them you have to see beyond the exterior and look inside. Not many of us truly wear our hearts on our sleeves especially in work environments and this can make understanding them a real challenge.

Blame cultures tend not to exist in environments populated by great people in part because they recognise that mistakes are often an inevitable part of pushing the boundaries and that the most important lesson to learn is not "who can we blame" but what can we learn from the experience and how can we do it better next time.

All in all being able to understand people is vital to assembling a team able to be the best in any given market. Mike helped us understand this and to create a culture where negative attitudes were not welcome – not actively frowned upon but just not really welcome. Over time as the culture took hold we actively tried to recruit "people like us" using a variety of techniques including i2i's very effective psychometric testing tool overseen by Mike's colleague at i2i-DNA, Keith Porter.

Interestingly the culture then naturally started to reinforce itself in that those uncomfortable with it left to find new jobs elsewhere leaving openings for us to bring in new personnel picked because they possessed the type of open, positive, highly effective personality that we were looking for.

Over time language became naturally more positive, mistakes became learning opportunities, new ideas and strategies bloomed and a great many grew in this exciting and encouraging environment. New ideas were tested, boundaries were pushed and I have no doubt that our customers really sensed it. We were seen not only as a good company to deal with but one who enjoyed what we did which I know rubbed off on them.

As part of the process we asked ourselves what we aspired to as managers. Over several months we defined this and took what we learned and created a 360° appraisal system based (this time with the help of i2i's Peter Woodruff) on these identified traits. Think about it –

we determined what we should be doing and then went out and asked everyone if they thought we were measuring up. The key however was to act on the results, which we did. I can think of one "dyed in the wool" older manager who thought that interacting with the staff meant giving them a damn good dressing down. His first appraisal was dire but he had enough within himself to accept this, understand the way the world was changing and over time he became a key and much respected member of the team – the complete opposite of what he had been.

Looking back it was a great journey. I and many others learnt so much. We didn't always get it right but we treated people with respect, understood them, valued their contributions and made them part of a business that was seen as a role model - one that operated at a level many still aspire to - and for that I thank a chance meeting with Mike Finnigan and his team at i2i.

Jeremy Gorick, Entrepreneur

COALS TO NEWCASTLE

Mike's Introduction

Jan wanted to write up her own story using thoughts and questions given to her by us. The result was so powerful that we included it without any need for a second draft. Jan writes as she speaks, we can almost see her telling this story to us, and she is a lady of presence, eloquence and warmth, who balances her ability to inspire people with subtle strength.

Jan now lives with her husband Stan and her dogs in Florida, USA, and we have had many conversations with her over the phone at ridiculous times of the day, about her life and the exciting future that she is creating, but we never really understood the deep background to the story. We hope it touches you as it has us.

Jan's Story for Michael!

To say that I was overweight as a child is an understatement. By the time I was two years old I was tall, big boned, and chubby. In the fourth grade I weighed as much as my teacher. In the sixth grade, people thought I was my father's wife because I was so big – I did not look like a 12 year old at all. When I was thirteen I remember visiting the doctors for medication to speed up my metabolism. My teenage years were difficult. I tried every conceivable type of diet but nothing worked - it was a roller coaster of ups and downs.

At age 22, I was engaged to be married and in preparation for our wedding I stopped eating so that I could lose weight to fit into a 'small' wedding gown. I did get down to a size 12 in three months but I was fainting and not losing in a healthy, safe way. For that one moment in time, however, I was a size 12 – an event not to be repeated in over 32 years.

As expected, shortly after my wedding I gained everything back and then some. That's when I gave up. I told myself that I was born to be fat. I had inherited genes from my grandmothers and there was simply nothing that I could do! I would never diet again!

As the years went by, however, my health began to suffer. At age 40 I had a life-threatening illness that was brought on by my obesity. The doctor told me that I had to lose weight before I could expect to have my problems resolved and that if I couldn't get my weight down my illness would escalate. I sought help and dieted for eight months, until my health was restored. Then I went back to the old patterns and habits for the next 14 years. I knew that at some point my life-long history of obesity would catch up to me but there was nothing I could do to prevent it.

In July, 2000, at the age of 53, I had high blood pressure, Type II diabetes (non-insulin dependent), shortness of breath, and heart palpitations. My back ached constantly; my knees were always in pain. I would sleep for only a few hours each night and then lie awake wondering how much longer I would live because I was afraid that my health was beyond repair. I felt so sickly that I was convinced that I wouldn't make it another week.

Finally, I made the decision to seek out a new doctor...a specialist in metabolism and endocrinology. Perhaps a new physician with expertise in these areas could help me – maybe, just maybe, he had the key to losing weight.

My first visit confirmed everything that I had thought – my health was out of control. The doctor told me that if I continued on the path that I had been following for all of these years he was sure I would not live to be an old woman to enjoy life with my husband and my family. He also told me that all of my health problems were a result of my obesity and that if I lost weight my health would improve considerably. These were not the words I wanted to hear. He had no miracle cure. He was telling me that I had a lot of work to do.

I remember thinking that he had no idea of how hard this was going to be. Why, I had been fat all of my life. I couldn't change how I lived, how I ate, how the gene pool affected me! There was no way . . . I was obese . . . it was a fact of life. But, I really had no choice. If I didn't do something NOW I would have no future. I was convinced that I would not be successful but to appease the doctor, I would give it a go. And, if my past history was any indication, this would be a temporary situation. When my health improved, I could go off my diet. So very reluctantly, with great fear and trepidation, I started to count my calories.

I set a limit of 1200 calories a day . . . surely this would make me lose tons of weight very quickly. During the first three weeks I was so impressed with myself. I lost 14 pounds. While it was a drop in the bucket, it was still encouraging. I calculated how many months it would take for me to get down to a goal weight. If I could keep losing at the rate of 4.6 pounds a week it would not take that long after all.

Now, of course, I had deluded myself by thinking this was going to be easy and that I would only have to diet for a short period of time.

My body rebelled and set me straight – it told me that I was on my own; it was not going to be cooperative and it would not make this an easy task. In the fourth and fifth week of my calorie counting, faithfully staying on track, I didn't lose an ounce. Depression set in and I was angry.

Why couldn't I have been born with 'skinny genes'? Excuse after excuse set in. I convinced myself that I couldn't do it . . . there was no way I could succeed. But I promised to give it one more week so that I could at least tell the doctor that I tried.

At the end of the sixth week, I gained four pounds. I had faithfully counted every calorie, had starved myself for the past three weeks and then actually gained four pounds. Impossible! Later, when I asked professionals for advice, I was told that my body thought it was starving to death so it was trying to preserve me. Now, really! If you had seen me at that point you would have been well assured that I was not starving to death.

Interestingly enough, the discovery of my four-pound weight gain was on the first morning of a three-day program called, **'Peak Performance Through Positive Thinking'** – intriguing title. I was asked to evaluate the program, presented by Mike Finnigan, for my employer to see what I thought of it and how we could use it to help employees improve their performance and results. Of course, family, friends and work mates always commented on my high performance and positive thinking, so I thought there was probably nothing applicable to me but I was willing to 'evaluate it for the Company'.

I will tell you that when I left the house that morning I was not in a good frame of mind. Actually I was livid. I had lost control totally. I gained four pounds. Out of anger and frustration, I promised myself I would eat everything laid out during the day – muffins, lunch, desert, afternoon cookies, a chocolate elephant, if one was offered. I didn't care. The diet was not working. My health would have to suffer. And if I didn't live to be an old lady, so be it – I would live a short life but not have to count calories ever again. I was fat and that's all there was to it. There was no way I could successfully diet - I tried and look where it got me. I was too old to change; I had been this way for 53 years and that was how it was going to be. I was a product of my genetic inheritance and there was nothing I could do about it.

Yes, I walked into the program that morning with every excuse in the book raging through my mind - Michael Finnigan had no idea that I was his challenge for the day! **And little did I know it would change my life!**

As the program began, Michael's enthusiasm and energy soon became contagious.

By lunchtime, we learned about 'dendrites' and the physiology of our minds. As we went through the day, I learned that even though patterns and habits are imbedded in our minds and that we cannot rid ourselves of them, we *can* create new ones. If we focus on specific thoughts repeatedly, we create new patterns, new dendrites which enlarge with repeated use: the bigger the dendrites the better, because the new ones lead our minds down the path of least resistance, which in this case would be the new, positive pattern. This in turn allows us to make the right decisions.

Then we started talking about the creative sub-conscious mind and the fact that it provides consistency whether it is good for us or not. When I learned that it acts as we instruct it to do so, I began to understand how my thoughts were affecting me. I will confess that it all made sense but as much as I wanted to believe it, I was still very skeptical. Could I really do this? Was it possible? Could I change my thought patterns and subsequently my behaviour?

Day two convinced me that I could do it! I realized that for all of these years I continually engaged in negative self-talk when it came to dieting. To change my behaviour I had to change my self-talk. The strangest thing of all was the fact that I was always perceived by others to be an extremely optimistic, positive person. Yet when it came to focusing on myself, I was negative . . . always driving, pushing, trying to be perfect in those areas where I felt I could excel. In areas where I felt I had no control, I put them aside, ignored them and then berated myself because of it. Since I always thought I could not control my weight, I didn't! It was time for a change. I had to think, feel, and talk myself into the fact that I could do it!

Later in the day, we discussed what it takes to succeed. The points I recall that had the greatest impact on me were that *desire was the key to success*. We need to *focus on the goal, not the tasks*. And, if we can *picture what we want*, it could drive us to remarkable results despite temporary defeats.

Immediately a mental picture of what I wanted to achieve came to mind. It was an old photograph of me, on that one day in time when I was a size 12.

I saw it; I felt it, and I was living that moment in time again.

That was my goal — to fit into the dress I was wearing in the photo - a dress that for some reason I had kept tucked away in an old trunk in the attic for all of these years. It was all up to me and I had the power to make changes in my life. I could create new dendrites that would be larger and stronger than the old.

Michael promised, 'When your dream is more powerful than the obstacle, it will come true.' That did it! I started positive self-talk and did not stop! I could not get the photograph out of my mind. I knew that it was going to take work but as long as I focused on my goal, I would handle the tasks one at a time even when I had temporary setbacks. I started building dendrites a mile wide and a mile deep.

That night when I got home, I shared my notes and thoughts with my husband, Stan. He was encouraged by my enthusiasm and I spent several hours over the weekend coming up with a plan. I couldn't stop thinking about what I had learned and that photograph kept popping into my mind. I didn't waste any time putting the plan into action.

On Monday, I joined a weight management program and now I am eating in a healthy, balanced way - and in a manner that I can live with the rest of my life.

My body is not always cooperative and there are weeks when I gain a pound, but I remember that these are 'temporary setbacks' and I focus on my goal to stay on track. The most amazing thing is I no longer get angry at these setbacks and threaten to give up. I tell myself that by maintaining my focus, the next weigh-in will give me the results I want. If I choose to eat something that is not on my balanced, nutritional food plan I no longer beat myself up over it. I enjoy it and then move on. What is most surprising is that I no longer crave my former pattern of eating. It's the new, healthy choices that I enjoy the most. My new dendrite is working!

I continue to visit the doctor every three months; he has been a great encouragement to me. His directness and honesty help me maintain discipline and his affirmation that my actions have impacted my health in a positive way, only fortify my desire for success.

Stan has been a great support and has joined me in the efforts to lose weight. Just a few weeks ago he told me that he knows I will achieve my goal because my mental attitude is different than ever before. He overheard me talking to someone who was bemoaning the fact that dieting meant you had to give up everything you liked. My response was, 'I have not given up anything. I just choose to eat something else for today.'

Sharing my experience and verbalizing my goals with others has also helped. The more I talk about my experiences the more they understand my motivation and what has made me change my thinking. People who have known me for years comment about the physical changes resulting from my weight loss, but more importantly, they recognize that my attitude is different – that something in my head has changed!

My constant focus on what I learned in 'Peak Performance Through Positive Thinking' has made a major impact on my ability to make decisions and face challenges daily. It has also impacted my professional life as well – I am applying what I learned to every facet of my life with incredible results.

During the months since, my professional role has changed significantly.

There were major stresses in my job and choices to be made but I have managed them well and have a strong, positive attitude about what I am doing. I have made a total career change taking on a new role that offers me the ability to explore and develop my creative talents. It was a role I had thought about for years but never had the courage to take on. Recently, my manager thanked me for my efforts and told me that he was impressed with what I had accomplished. He also expressed that he was pleasantly surprised that I was able to maintain a positive attitude through all of the changes that have gone during this time.

I have developed a list of goals for the future and have begun to work toward achieving them. Every so often someone will raise an eyebrow at the list for not all of these goals are 'conventional'. But it's reassuring to know that I WILL ACHIEVE THEM. There are no doubts in mind! I can picture it; I can feel it; I can do it! For the first time in my life I have confidence in my ability to do anything that I desire to do.

How am I doing? Absolutely fantastic! In the last ten months I have lost 55 pounds. I am five sizes smaller than when I began! My doctor now complains that I am healthier than he is! My blood pressure is no longer high and my blood sugars are better than normal. I can walk without being short of breath.

My medications have been cut in half and I will not need them at all after my next doctor's visit in two months.

I sleep through the night now and on those rare occasions when I wake early in the morning, I think about all of the things I am going to accomplish in my life when I am 70, 80 or 90!

Of course, Stan will still be with me because he has lost 42 pounds and has improved his health as well! Is this powerful or what?

As for my size 12 dress, it's not in the attic any more. I've taken it out of the storage chest, cleaned and pressed it. It's waiting for me! I expect it will take me another year before it fits. But that's okay . . . for, you see, I am not dieting any longer . . . I have chosen a new way of life and know that I will succeed.

Continued support from the 'twins' Michael Finnigan and Andrew O'Donoghue who are my 'coaches' and dear friends, has made an incredible difference in my life. They inspire me and fill my life with positive thoughts!

RELATE AND ASSIMILATE

Jan is no different to many people who come through the i2i programme; at first, she was cynical about the course, and she was also despondent at her inability to resolve a lifelong issue. She also truly was a positive person already, so her peers were right. So what did she teach me?

1 That, to quote Bob Champion, 'all battles can be won'. Jan faced a massive fight for her health, indeed her life, which she had been losing for decades. She taught me that there is ALWAYS hope, and that we should never give in on any goal we set.

2 That people who are often initially cynical about our course, and in fact about this material as a whole, often gain the most.

3 That to achieve true success, you keep your eye on your goal and off any temporary setbacks you may have along the way.

Jan is a great achiever, and we share a friendship now, across thousands of miles, which is very special.

Thank you, Jan

PS. Jan, as she expected, no longer takes insulin following that subsequent visit to the doctor!

What did Jan teach you?

1

2

3

Jan's Story

"I can picture it; I can feel it; I can do it !! "

THE GOLDEN FIND

Mike's Introduction

This was an amazing interview. Here I was sitting with the Chairman of a successful company, who was telling me that our principles had changed his life! Listen carefully to the way Rod talks about his early years in business and reveals 'the hardest task facing any entrepreneur'. He tells how he learned the 'do's and don'ts' of motivating people, and the power of stamping out 'blame cultures'.

Mike	*So, Rod some time in 1999 you must have got a marketing letter from us.*
Rod	I did yes; I think that in 1999 I received quite a number of marketing shots from you!
Mike	*Yes you would get a few before we give up!*
Rod	They were impressive in themselves, but I think it was the tie-up between Paul Heathcote and the Preston North End venue that got me hooked. I attended your breakfast seminar there in June, led by Andrew. There were about 20 or so business people from around the area, and I really just bought in to it. I'd gone through a situation in May of that year which caused me to start to analyse where I had been going wrong in business terms.
Mike	*You were successful already though.*
Rod	I was successful in generating turnover; not so successful in the previous two years in creating profitability. I actually took three months out of the business, apart from doing the routine stuff that came across my desk. I worked seven days a week spending every available moment, cataloguing the areas where I'd thought had the answers and looking at the mistakes I'd made over the period.

I discovered that I had surrounded myself with the wrong type of people by and large; weak people, who wouldn't give me honest and open feedback. I decided what I thought we needed to do to move the whole thing back in the right direction.

I was the prime mover in the business, but it was now a business with over 20 offices and it could no longer move ahead with just my efforts alone.

I knew I needed a strong management team - I never had that before.

I had had a poor group managing director previously, who I'd promoted from regional management level over a number of years. I wasn't analytical about people. When I recruited senior people they came in and all I wanted to give them was a fancy story about how well the company was doing; about how we were winners. I never really looked at people; never really studied them and looked at their track records.

So I set about coming out with a list of four people that I needed to actually help me turn the business around; the senior team.

After seeing you in action, I got the main 11 people in the business together; the core team of five senior directors, our human resources manager, and a series of sales people and regional managers. We spent a weekend away with Andrew - that was in the September.

During the session, from my point of view, it was all the experiences of life that were shared that really opened so many doors for me, in terms of why I'd become who I was. I was basically insecure; but because I was an entrepreneur I thought I was a natural people person. I'd always believed I was a people person; I'd always believed that, because I had this knack and this ability to be able to meet with people, sell to them, convince them to put their trust in me and commit their business to me.

In reality, I was the furthest thing from a people person, because I had no interest in people when it came down to it because of my own insecurity. I only could judge on the basis of what people could bring to me financially. **Success, in my terms, was 'the bottom line'** as it is with so many entrepreneurs. So many of them have charm and charisma, but beyond a certain size they become almost their own worst enemy in a business sense.

The trick that actually makes things happen, the ability to lead people through the dark, is no real issue in the first few years.

This is because if you're a reasonable entrepreneur you have got the ability to sell; and you're so successful, that people are prepared to put up with the issues.

But those same people can exist in fear - in a total 'fear factor' scenario - all the time. An entrepreneur is all powerful. He's not used to taking 'no' for an answer; he doesn't want to listen to people; to give them a fair hearing. He surrounds himself with people who are genuinely subservient to him, because he's the person who is making all this happen, creating all the wealth and these people are just carried along on the shirt tails; that's how it is in the early stages.

Now, when a company expands, that's when the problems begin. I almost doubled the size of the company overnight by buying another business, which had a £14 million turnover. I tried to merge that with the existing business and, it was like trying to merge oil and water – two completely different cultures.

I started the business in 1990 and by 1994 it was a winning culture. Nobody wanted to leave the company; there were no issues; we were hiring people; we were making a name for ourselves in the marketplace; people were on big profit shares; everyone was getting bonuses at year-end. It was a win–win.

It was only then, as we grew, that the fact that I didn't have a management team was exposed. I divided to conquer, and denigrated people's positions. I undermined them and was doing all the wrong things, and that really caused major, major problems in the business.

From that moment on, whilst sales continued to move upwards, the profitability went down from £712,000 profit, to almost a break-even situation three years after. Attrition rates amongst staff were something like 70-80%; the morale was incredibly low, and even though looking back all that was obvious, nobody gave me that feedback.

Eventually, though, I was beginning to realise that I had to work on my behaviour and really do something with regards to the staff attrition levels in the business.

Your programme made me realise that as a child I could only ever really remember being criticised. Whether Dad was watching me play football or whether it was about my homework, it was always, 'You could have run a bit faster, tackled a bit harder, done a bit better'. It was all negative, never praise or encouragement - really it was just survival for me.

Yet I also remember the love at home that was freely given by my mum. We were six boys and she brought us up on her own. Dad gave us no emotional support. Mum brought us up and did all the washing, cleaning, cooking, everything! On the course I began to recognise my Dad in me; in the things I did with my children; where I was creating in them this 'self-fulfilling prophecy'. Unless you can break this mould, and change your behaviour, it will just continue. I do wish I had had a different upbringing, yet I also realise that the drive I have to succeed in business does come from my insecurity, and the search for recognition.

Mike   *So, on the course, you were thinking of yourself as the whole person, not just the business man?*

Rod   Definitely. Andrew asked us all to sum up the impact at the end of the course and that was what I said - that it was like somebody opening a door for me, and showing me how I could actually change the way I reacted; and that's what I did.

After the course I basically set out to do three things, and I have never until now told anybody else what these are, and these were:

1 to actually pause for five seconds before I react to a situation; to look at things as positively as I could

2 to never again judge success by financial measures only

3 to adopt a more positive and supportive attitude to family and colleagues

Those were my three things. It is easier now than it was at first, because they were all things I had never done. They were simple things, but I think about them every time I have a conversation, whether that is in a board meeting or, more importantly, with my family.

Mike   *Have people noticed a change in you?*

Rod   You go and ask! They all relate to that course that I have talked about over and over again.

Speak to any of them, my wife or whoever, and they will say what a marked change there was in me; and this is not just hype. It was real; you made a difference to me, and I felt it, it was powerful.

It came at the right time for me. Everyone gave positive feedback from every aspect of the course, and one of them stopped smoking and still has stopped! She heard Andrew's example of his former love for chocolate, and thought that if he could make that change, then so could she with cigarettes.

It also worked with me in stopping me getting colds, which I always used to get; it worked in my golf. I have become a better golfer. If you approach a putt with any amount of negativity whatsoever, there is a very good chance, say 85%, that you will miss that putt. If you go with a positive attitude, you lower that percentage. I'm playing consistently to my handicap, which is down one. On average a golfer plays to his handicap two or three times a year - I now play to mine regularly. I'm striking the ball well, and enjoying my golf again.

I won a competition recently because of my new ability to play consistently, and that is just down to my attitude!

And I suppose people will look at me and say I should have a positive attitude, but 18 months ago I didn't have. And I still have to work at it. You know at the end of the day, this is not a panacea, but it shows you that there is a different way, a better way, of thinking.

It teaches you, I suppose like Richard Branson's background did, to believe in yourself, to try things, to know no fear.

Mike   *I have met several people who work with him, and they all talk about him with great warmth, because he believes in them, and frees them to go and do their best.*

Rod   Yes, and he has faced extinction in business a few times, but that attitude and strength of character carried him through.

Mike   *In an interview with Martin Lewis he listed his favourite quality in people as 'forgiveness'.*

Rod   But Mike, if you can get a 'no blame' culture into a business, I think you are 85% on the right road.

Our approach in the early stages was 'heads on poles' and the insecurity that creates is criminal. It devastates a culture. You have people who hate working there; they are constantly oppressed and monitored, and I am talking about some big businesses here, not just entrepreneurs. It was insecurity on my part that caused it for me, but if the profit was not right I would be looking for somebody's head! I used to call each office every Friday; the best would be congratulated and the worst berated.

I should have been looking for ways in which I could help. I am now more human, and I thank you and Andrew for that. I have been in business for 20 years, and it's only now that I have learned what you really need to do. Most companies don't survive ten years, and it's no wonder with the entrepreneurial trait, which manifests itself in poor management and succession planning. I did so much damage in my own way. I had never been trained as a manager; I was a draughtsman!

Mike	*You have committed a lot of resource to our programme, presumably because you have seen benefits not just for you?*
Rod	Well, look at Tom, who runs 'Cash Friday' *(one of Rod's businesses)*; he's the same age as me, and he committed straight away after he had been through the course! I did too, but didn't want to impose it on anyone. None of the other managing directors did – they thought it would be too complicated for their managers, too intensive, too much to take in!

But Tom committed to put ALL his people through. **When he went on that course his business was making £300,000 and it's now making over a million!** So, he wasn't doing a lot wrong there was he? Now, I think Tom was more of a manager than I was anyway, more logical and reflective, more balanced. So, for us it has been a golden find, it really has. |
Mike	*I hope this will really strike a chord with people Rod, what do you think?*
Rod	Mike, your course gives people a wonderful opportunity. If they can buy into the fact that I have overcome these problems because of it, I hope that will be beneficial to them. If I had had this balanced view of business that I have now, I would have been far more successful than I am now: far more successful.
Mike	*Why?*
Rod	Because for so many years, as this interview indicates, I have worked against my own interests! I didn't know I was doing it at the time – I was blissfully ignorant. I think that it is typical of entrepreneurs, to go through an early Survival period. A Survival period then changes into a Strategic period – and this is the most difficult transition, because the skill sets are different.

Finding a way to make the transition is crucial. The programme made me realise that and showed me what I needed to do and should have done earlier. I hope others who may be reading this and who are in a similar situation can accept that.

The Jimmy White story was a powerful one for me; the most extreme example of a person pushing success away; but by degree that is what I was like, and what many people are like.

I have to pinch myself now sometimes. I see so much insecurity around now, but I understand it now; so much fear, so much |

stress. For me, working with you guys, and having strong people who give me feedback has helped so much. Those things stop me reverting back under pressure.

I also wanted to send all my family on the course! It made such an impact on me as a person.

I just hope people will buy into all that.

RELATE AND ASSIMILATE

What a sincere and humble man Rod is. He talks gently, yet with real insight, and truly believes that working with us has helped him change his life. He called us his 'Golden Find' and I think I know what he means, but he did teach me:

1   To be humble about success. The humility staves off complacency, and also means you are unlikely to be perceived as being arrogant by others.

2   To run a business based on values including trust, mutual respect, empowerment for people, and honesty. Rod often talks about the need for feedback, and how successful people create a culture where that can be given and taken securely.

3   That if you want a profitable business, keep your eye on the values, processes, habits and happiness of the people; then the profits will come.

Thanks Rod, great, great lessons.

What were the top three lessons you learned from Rod?

1

2

3

If you want a successful business, keep your eye on the values, processes, habits and happiness of the people, and the profits will come.

'OK, WHAT DO WE DO NOW?'

Mike's Introduction

Helen talks in this interview about her fight against a life threatening illness and shares with you the secret of her discovery; for the first time in her life she found an amazing fighting spirit which saw her through.

Helen and her husband Barry are so deserving of our admiration for the way in which they fought their battle.

This is the story of one amazing woman.

Mike   *So you must have been one of the very first people to attend the course?*

Helen   Yes, I was. It was at a school hall in Preston.

Mike   *Yes, I remember - my girls' junior school, St Oswald's. Andrew must have asked you to come.*

Helen   I've always been interested in that type of thing. But I really can't remember how it came about - although Andrew's wife Jacqui is one of my closest friends. It was at a time in my life when I wasn't really doing very much career wise and I was stuck at home looking after the children. I suppose I was hoping for some kind of inspiration to help see where I was going and that's all I can remember about it really.

Mike   *It must have been a weird experience sitting in a school hall, on small chairs with small desks looking like 11 year olds, which is what I remember of it.*

Helen   There were only about six or seven people and we all got on really well. It was great to see them all again a few weeks later, to see how they were getting on.

I've had a few issues with my life when I've thought "Where do I go now? What do I do?" I've given up my career to have the children but I do want something. Barry had started his business so he was up and out and sort of being ambitious and doing all the things he wanted to do and I was kind of left - you know, 'what do I do now' type of thing.

So I was looking for something and the course inspired me really to explore new options and new opportunities.

I was looking for something and almost immediately after I finished the course a direct sales opportunity came up, so I thought I'd give it a try.

Tablets of Stone 1
If you have nothing to lose by trying and everything to gain, then by all means try

W Clement Stone

Mike   *Would you not have tended to do that before?*

Helen   No, I wouldn't, because I've never been in sales before; I have a medical background, but no experience of office work, sales and business – no business experience whatsoever! Still, I thought 'this sounds good fun. I'm going to go out and give it a go' and from the moment I went out there I was really very successful immediately, and I sort of shocked myself. It made me realise that I could do things that I hadn't previously thought that I could do.

Mike   *Direct sales is one of the hardest things you can possibly do! I would never have said that to you at the time, but it is, in reality, a tough game.*

Helen   I found I learned very, very quickly. I wouldn't previously have believed that I had the personality to do it, but now I realised it had to be something to do with my new found attitude of believing that I could try something and be successful.

That was when I first realised that the course was working for me. It made a difference to my home life too, and so my husband Barry kept saying he would go on the course but he didn't have enough time.

I had had a history of depression as well so whenever I felt any feelings like that coming back in my life, I now had new methods and ways of dealing with them when I felt myself going down the slippery slope again.

Mike   *So using the new 'tools' made them go away?*

Helen   Yes, they do go away now. The course has given me confidence to talk to other people about it that have been in the same position. When I first had depression which was before I went on the programme I saw a counsellor and a lot of stuff came out.

I'd never told anyone because of the 'taboo' – but a lot of people suffer from depression at some time in their life and there are ways that you can pull yourself out of it.

Tablets of Stone 2
Meet the most important living person — YOU!

W Clement Stone

Mike   And ultimately only you will pull yourself out of it; the drugs won't help, they will just kill the pain; they won't actually make it go away.

It's up to you, however hard that is.

Helen   I know that now.

So, having got my life back into some order - an old hip problem came back. I've always had a problem with my hip ever since I was a teenager.

I was born with a congenital dislocation which we didn't find out about until I was almost three, when the damage had been done. Over the years I've been backwards and forwards to many doctors to try and find a solution. My fitness was going downhill with each passing year, and with having the children, I was starting to do less and less and become more and more unfit. Every time I went to find out what I could do about it, the doctor would recommend replacing the hip at fifty.

Mike   How old were you?

Helen   I was only in my 20's, so that got me down a few times. So, through positive thinking, I knew there had to be a solution, and one thing that the course taught me was that if you were forever looking for a solution or a way forward then it will come to you.

Almost by magic!

And I don't really know how it quite came about, but I went through different therapists, and eventually I found the perfect person for the job. He recommended an operation - rare and extreme. I had a choice to make then, because I had managed to live a reasonably normal life, but I was living with pain every day.

I knew it would put me out of action for a year, but I went ahead and had the operation and was very positive throughout, made a record recovery, and got back.

I got mobile again more quickly than you would have expected and I did really well **but then of course I found out I had**

cancer, which was a bit of a shock, because I was only off my crutches for a couple of weeks.

I wasn't completely back on my feet but I felt as though I was doing really well. To suddenly find out that I had cancer was a bit of a shock really but I do feel that the last few years leading up to me having cancer, the things that have happened in my life and the way my attitude has changed, prepared me for what was about to happen.

If I had found out five years previously that I had had cancer, it would have been absolutely devastating. Now though, instead of thinking, 'how the hell am I ever going to get out of this?' I felt that I had the ground work and preparation to deal with it.

I mean nobody likes it when you find out something like that, but you can either curl up and die and accept 'that's my life completely finished', or decide to fight. I'm sure that has a huge difference on the prognosis really and after the initial shock my thoughts were that I had to do something.

Mike   *So how long did it last, the initial shock, before you got round to thinking, 'come on I've got to do something'?*

Helen   Well the initial shock I would say only lasted a few minutes. I was absolutely hysterical when they told me – it's a woman's worst fear to have breast cancer.

They said I was to come in the following week for an operation, so I knew immediately we were not talking about a little lump. We were talking about something massive. My first thoughts were 'God, I'm going to die' but within a few minutes I shook myself out of it.

I cried obviously because it's a normal reaction but I thought 'I've got to be strong here' and 'I've got to be positive about it'. We were going to pick the children up straight after coming out of the doctor's office. So I sort of pulled myself round and thought 'I've just got to get on with it'. The next day we went back to see the doctor and it was a different person that walked in the room, a totally different person from the person that had been there the day before.

I said 'OK, what do we do now?'

He told us what would happen and that it would take a year for the treatment that I was going to have. He told me what was likely to happen, and he recommended we promised ourselves

38

a 'treat' at the end of the year. So that was December, and for the following December, we booked... a month in Australia! This had been something in my Life Plan. We've always wanted to go diving on the Great Barrier Reef.

Within a month of my diagnosis some friends of ours said they were moving to Australia. They were devastated because they had only just found out about my cancer when they were leaving , but they just said 'you must come and visit us'.

It almost felt like things were meant to happen; that things all came together - friends moving out there; the doctor saying 'organise yourself a treat at the end of all this, something to look forward to'. It was strange really.

I have to say the doctor was brilliant; a very positive person. He was fantastic and just said exactly the right things.

Mike   *With your hip, you found the right person, and there you are finding the right surgeon again!*

Helen   Yes and another funny thing was that he had only just moved to Bolton. He had only been there about two weeks, and he was the perfect person for me. He didn't hold anything back, but at the same time he was very positive.

Mike   *But even though you are talking about this surgeon you're not talking about his surgical ability - you're talking his attitude. It's the bedside manner that makes the difference between maybe a very good one and an outstanding one. That's what Patch Adams talks about. I know there are surgical skills involved, but you're talking about his ability to help you through, which is something else, isn't it?*

Helen   Yes it is, he kept me sane and Barry would agree with me. We came out feeling 'this guy knows what he is doing - there is not a problem' and 'if there is something that can be done, this is the man to do it'. So we took him at his word - we organised the treat for the following December and throughout the treatment we would talk about arranging what we were going to do when we were over there. It was all booked and sorted and I thought 'I'm going to be well - fit and well - on the day that we go'.

Mike   *You had this in your mind?*

Helen   Yes, I had this in my mind. I imagined us there. I imagined both the two of us slim and healthy, because we had both put on weight.

Mike	*And how is he doing by the way?*
Helen	You would not recognise him! I put on quite a bit of weight after my hip operation through not being able to exercise and before I got going again I started with my cancer treatment. Steroids make you put on weight so I sort of reached full maximum weight - and Barry did the same. We were both in sympathy with each other and maybe food was a comfort, I don't know.

So it was in my head when we went out to Australia we were going to 'knock 'em dead' and show them that if you can get through this you can get through anything.

At the end of my chemotherapy I was feeling pretty damned weary and not able to pull myself back quite as quickly as I thought I would be able to. The doctor told me that they were giving me a massive dose. I knew they were going to throw absolutely everything they could at me, so I mean, it doesn't get any worse.

A year had passed from my hip problem as well, and I was coming out of the feelings from the chemotherapy and the radiotherapy. My hip was starting to improve. It had niggled a bit throughout, but I started to exercise again and Barry and I went on a diet.

Now when we decide we are going to do something, if we want it enough, we just go for it. We both wanted to be slim and healthy going away for our holiday of a lifetime, so Barry lost three stones (you wouldn't recognise him!) and I lost over two stones - so we're both kind of at our ideal weight again.

Mike	*You look ten years younger now than when we first met four years ago! We've seen you throughout the illness, but if anybody ever met you now they'd have no idea what you have been through during those three years - no idea!*
Helen	And I'm really proud of that as well.
Mike	*I should think so.*
Helen	If you feel you are looking as good as you possibly can, it makes you feel well, and that has the effect of making you think, 'if I can do that and come out looking good after major surgery twice in six months and come out 12 months later looking even better than before, then wow!'

The power of positive thinking had a major influence on the way I dealt with all of this, and I do feel that getting involved in the course and the follow-up meetings was all preparation for what

	I was about to have to deal with, and I certainly went through it thinking 'if I can get through this I can handle anything'.
Mike	*So what was this Australian trip like then?*
Helen	Oh, the Australian trip! Well we went to Sydney and it was very, very hot. We saw our friends, who we get on really well with - they've actually lived with us before, and we just had the most amazing time.
	The children had the time of their lives, they got into the beach life, the school, meeting all the other local kids and everybody was so friendly. It was a completely different lifestyle.
Mike	*And what about you?*
Helen	Barry and I had a very relaxing time and we didn't want it to end.
	We saw everything we wanted to see and at the end of it our friends had the children stay with them while we went away for a few days on our own.
	We – although this was all prepared by me! – found the most exclusive villa. I took the Surgeon at his word in making it a 'real treat' and I investigated the best resorts. I found one of the top resorts in the world on the Great Barrier Reef – The Hayman Islands it was called – it was just unbelievable!
Mike	*So did you do the snorkelling?*
Helen	Yes, we went on the Great Barrier Reef.
Mike	*And the hip was fine?*
Helen	Well it's like I'm a teenager again! I'd say from the age of 17 onwards I had pain – and now I'm working out at the gym two or three times a week, I can walk a reasonable distance and I'm not feeling pain.
Mike	*That's incredible.*
Helen	Yes it is absolutely incredible, snorkelling on the Great Barrier Reef was easy - so next time we're going to try diving. We did lots of things including a helicopter ride over the island. It was fantastic - it was a real treat, a real wonderful treat and we knew the boys were happy and we were away for almost a month.
Mike	*Helen, looking back, we asked you to do so many thing. I gave you the Jason Gaes book, 'You don't have to die' and all those other things, and anything that we ever asked you to do you did. Some of the things that you went through, some of the*

lengths you went to! You are AMAZING. And then to get the **Bristol Cancer Help Centre**, *tell us about that.*

Helen   I was having chemotherapy at that time but I was still trucking up to the health club every day. I saw you one to one throughout the chemotherapy, which was fantastic; it helped me so much, just the top up to keep positive.

Mike   *We did two hour sessions once a month, planned in between the chemotherapy sessions so that we always met about two or three weeks before your next one?*

Helen   Yes that's right, it was sort of in between, when I was feeling well enough to come out.

But we looked at lots of different coping strategies because at the time I was trying to use the cold cap to prevent hair loss - which I managed to keep for four months although it was extremely painful. But what we did together really helped through that pain.

Mike   *You did some wacky things didn't you?*

Helen   We took the video machine to the hospital room so we could watch our favourite films in bed. The doctor thought I was a complete idiot he really did! Barry had this holdall, and each time I went for chemotherapy he loaded up with all sorts of stuff - aromatherapy oils, our favourite coffee and treats; all ideas we got from the meetings with you! He would read to me, massage my feet – all different things! And you just helped me come up with the ideas of how I could get through it.

Anyway, at the health club, I saw a girl one day and for some reason I felt like I wanted to talk to her. I didn't know her, I'd never met her before in my life, never even seen her there before, but she came over and sat with me. She must have picked up some sort of vibe; it was really quite bizarre but I just found out through talking with her – how it came up I don't really know I must have asked the right things or said the right things - that her husband had died of cancer six months earlier. She was an alternative therapist as well and she started talking about the Bristol Cancer Help Centre which you and I had only spoken about literally days before.

I'd never heard of it before so I sent off for lots of details from them. I'd looked at nutrition and all sorts of different things before and now I do intend to go and visit the centre. So that was one of the many coincidences that gave me the confidence to try other things.

I had reflexology throughout my treatment and that was something that gave me a lot of relaxation; and I used the therapy oils and Barry would massage me when I going through the treatment. All sorts of different things that I would have never have done before really helped.

Mike   *I remember we gave you a smiley face mouse mat to cover the clock up didn't we!*

Helen   Yes I had kept looking at the clock and when the doctor came in there was all these comedy videos – and a smiley face instead of a clock!

Mike   *I often wondered, when I used to think of you trundling off with all this stuff, what impact it would have if other people would do the same thing. Would it have made their stay a bit more pleasant or seem a bit shorter? You wonder don't you if that was the case. It was phenomenal you worked so hard at all that.*

Helen   Yes I did work very hard and I was very proud.

Mike   *Did you have this powerful vision at the end, was there anything else that you were focusing on or was Australia the main thing?*

Helen   It was really just coming out of it 'well', without being completely . . . well without looking like I had been dragged through a bush! I wanted to come out of it with some dignity and knowing that this wasn't a death sentence.

Mike   *And you wrote your i2i 'Inevitable Dreams' (IDs)?*

Helen   My self-talk has always been fantastic- and my IDs included what I was going be doing in a certain period of time.

Mike   *So what's the goal now then – what's the next one or is it a secret?*

Helen   Well, so many positive things have come out of this illness, which sounds really quite bizarre, I've been able to change my lifestyle and I feel now that I've got this big open space of opportunities to really find out where I want to be and what I want to do. I wouldn't have had that if I hadn't had all the traumas. My lifestyle is the best it has ever been.

Mike   *It's an amazing, fantastic story. Whoever you are and whatever trouble faces you, if you look for an answer you'll find it. That's what you said before. I believe that so implicitly and you must believe it.*

Helen   Imagine things you want to happen to you and they will happen. I can't really explain it anymore than that.

When you are facing your mountain, do the same as Helen, keep your eye on what you want, and you will be ready when the magic happens!

RELATE AND ASSIMILATE

Helen faced the toughest of obstacles by learning to think positively, and in doing so she found strength and courage she did not know she had. Barry helped her, and she found expert help in doctors, surgeons and therapists, like our great friend Dr Rosy Daniel in Bristol.

To me though, Helen helped herself. She used the tools we gave her, and therefore gave herself a fighting chance, which was all the experts needed.

When you are facing your mountain, do the same. Keep your eye on what you want, and you will be ready when the magic happens!

What did you learn from Helen's story?

1

2

3

AUTOPILOT

Mike's Introduction

Neil and I met for the first time in Harrogate, England, where he was with eleven other colleagues, including two people from the USA.

As a young man, Neil was an outstanding swimmer, and in this interview, he talks about getting back into the sport after a LONG break. The key to Neil's success, in my opinion, is his ability to use the goal setting tools we gave him. Neil does this as well as anyone I have ever met. We can learn so much from Neil about this. Watch how many times he mentions his goals (which we sometimes refer to as 'Inevitable Dreams').

Neil also shows how the tools for positive thinking bring positive results in all areas of life, and how results in your personal life build your confidence to apply the tools at work, with customers and colleagues.

I particularly enjoy Neil's stories about the record-breaking swimmer, and his son's spelling!

Whether you are a lapsed athlete, out of condition thirty (or forty or fifty) something, or frustrated parent, colleague or boss, Neil - the pupil turned teacher has a message for you.

Mike	*Neil, you came on our course in August 2000. Tell us what happened.*
Neil	Prior to the course, I had joined a health club as I hadn't done much exercise for a long time.
Mike	*How old are you now?*
Neil	I am 36. When I stopped running I was 16; that was probably the last regular exercise I had taken apart from the occasional game of squash. So I had thought for quite a while about getting back into shape. I joined a health club in June and I thought 'why not start swimming again?' So, I had a few lengths of the pool and got 'knackered' after 10 lengths as you might expect. I had half an idea that I would start competing again. I started to train but got fed up and stopped. That was mid July. I had lived with it for three weeks and just said 'forget it!'
	Then on the 3-day course you spoke about the power of dreams, self talk, the self image, and all that kind of good stuff and I thought, 'well okay . . .'
Mike	*Was all that new to you?*
Neil	Yes! Brand new! Usual management courses you go on speak

about techniques, process and all that kind of stuff, **but very few of those techniques actually impact the way you think.** They are very much 'out of a book' mentality – but what we learned from your course is that you must take a step back from all that, and understand how your mind works and what you can do with your mind to achieve what you always dreamed of. The powerful thing for me was the goal setting; again the normal technique was of saying 'I will do this' or 'I will do that'. The technique that you taught is to say 'I have done this.'

Mike   *Exactly! Put yourself there!*

Neil   Yes, imagine what it felt like; imagine the kind of reaction I am getting from those around me when I have done it. That alone was fantastic for me!

So as a result of the course I worked with some 'Inevitable Dreams', some work related and a few social ones. For example, one was to do the house up. That was just fantastic. I'd stalled on it for ages and finished it completely in no time at all after meeting you! Unbelievable!

Anyway, the swimming one was pretty clear, because prior to the course I had always said 'right I am going to do this' and I had always failed. After the course, I thought, 'Neil, what are you playing at? Get your backside into gear, set yourself a goal and get on with it! Go do it!'

So, one ID was swimming in the National Championships, having not done it for 20 years, and with no training at all! The National Championships were in Sheffield on 29th October, some three months after being on the course, so I had from August to the end of October. I just thought 'well, I'll try it – how much pain can it be?'

The key thing was to get my style back because obviously it is like riding a bike, you do not forget how to swim.

Mike   *Now, as a kid you were, an outstanding county swimmer, weren't you?*

Neil   Well, I never used to be able to get better than third in the county. I would be fastest in training, fastest in the heats and when it came to the crunch in the final, something would snap and I would never be able to do it!

Guys that I knew who were not as good as me would end up beating me on the day, to win the medals, the cups and all that. I have a tray at home full of silver and bronze, the largest selection of silver and bronze on the planet!

So, I started doing some stroke technique straight after the course. I was back in the pool, getting up at 6.15 in the morning and in the pool by 6.30, for an hour, and then I would go back home, get changed and go to work. I did not set myself that as a goal; I did not say that I would get into the pool at 6.30 in the morning and do an hour's training.

Mike   *I see - that just happened did it?*

Neil   Yes. The goal was, 'I have just swum 100 metres, I have recorded this great time, my family are in the balcony laughing and smiling, and I feel great!' That is the only goal that I set.

Mike   *Neil, from starting to say that to yourself every day, how long was it before this power kicked in that made you get out of bed at 6.15 every day?*

Neil   It was about a week. You come off the course and are pretty high anyway. That is the danger of any course – you stay high for a couple of days, but then you start to wane and get back into the drudgery of life.

Mike   *So, you then have to keep yourself high.*

Neil   Yes you do and you showed us how to do that.

The day after the course I was straight in the pool and I thought 'let's go for it'. The high lasted for a week, and that was all it needed to last for, because by then everything had kicked in and I was just on **autopilot**!

Probably without exception, every day from the end of the course until the championship I was in the pool. It was quite interesting that during the week you tend to get other people in the pool too, perhaps a couple of older gentlemen, older ladies, who go into the pool in the morning, maybe in their mid 60s, and they are going along gently, with their heads out of the water, not wanting to get their hair wet. So I started off doing breast stroke. I didn't want to make too many waves and splash them too much!

I thought I would do this and get my stroke back, and so I spent probably a couple of months doing breast stroke. One goal that I set when I was training was to get my number of strokes down per length, (if you can get the number of strokes down per length AND increase your repetition rate, then you can go faster).

When I started swimming breaststroke again, back in August, I was doing 11 strokes per length in a 25 metre pool, and I thought I would get it down to five.

Mike   *Hold on! Five in 25 metres, that's five metres per stroke?*

Neil   That's right. But by mid September I was down to six and I thought, 'this one has kicked in no problems at all!' I knew then that I would be down to five by the time of the championships. I got it sorted pretty quickly. When I started, I was only doing 20 lengths and I was absolutely knackered, yet within two weeks, I was up to about 45 lengths, and within a month I was doing about a mile and a half each day! It was incredible.

I lost a stone in about two months. My wife was pretty scared because I have always had a bit of a 'belly' and it was getting bigger as I went along and then, one day she said to me, 'where has your belly gone?' All I had been doing was swimming and she didn't believe me!

'You can't get a six pack from swimming!' she said.

Anyway, I was always a freestyle swimmer when I was a kid. So, when by September I was comfortable with my breaststroke, I started to think about entering the National Masters Championships. I'll tell you how that happened as well, because it was quite amazing to even get into the damned thing.

Now my freestyle goal kicked in, I am going to start splashing all these poor people in the water! So rather than do that to them, I started doing more work at the weekends, as nobody gets out of bed at 6.30 in the morning at weekends! So I used to be knocking on the door at 6.30am on Saturdays and Sundays and do two hours worth of freestyle. During the week I concentrated on my breaststroke with just a bit of freestyle. So that meant the freestyle got trained as well and I did a similar sort of thing as regards the stroke per length.

I started at 25 strokes per length and said 'right I'll halve it'. So by then I was down to 12 per length and thought 'now is the time I need some professional help'.

This is probably the beginning of September, about six weeks after the course. So I was looking on the internet for what kind of times I should be doing for my age group; I was feeling pretty good about what I had done and wanted to take a look at what I would need to do to achieve the top ten position I wanted to get.

I looked on the internet at the top ten best times for my age group and I thought 'I have a shot at this, and after not having done anything for 20 years, I can get into the top ten in the country'. The top ten does not sound very significant but when you have not done anything for the last 20 years, it is.

I was never anywhere near the top ten when I was a kid. I was third in the county, which equates to top 20 if you are lucky. So I thought I would get some professional help.

I looked at some of the events that were coming up and I emailed the girl that was organising one of them, asking how I got into it - I really wanted to do this.

So she sent the entry form to me and the only criteria is that to enter you have to be a member of a swimming club and you have to have been a member for a month prior to the event. I had two weeks to join a swimming club and get registered so I could enter this competition. I thought 'I'll blow it if I'm not careful. I'm going to run out of time!' That night when I got this response back, saying I needed to get sorted out with a club, I started phoning around in a blind panic.

Again I was looking on the internet for other competitions that were around - there was one which I noted was being organised by my old swimming coach when I was a kid in Birmingham and there was a phone number there for him. So, I phoned him up - he was 55 now and I had not spoken to him for at least 24 years!

So, I phoned him up and said, 'Hello Andy, how are you doing?' He could not believe it! So I told him what I was doing and I told him I had been training for this event and that I wanted to get into breast stroke and freestyle and I really wanted to get into the National Masters in Sheffield and I needed to join a swimming club. I said to him, 'Look, I don't care how I do it, but I need to do it!' (There is nothing round here - Stockport area - I could have joined the Stockport Metro Club, but I could never train with them because they don't get out of bed early enough in the mornings!) So he explained that he ran a Masters Swimming Club down in Birmingham.

So I went down to Birmingham that weekend to see him and he took me along to his swimming club, which was called FHM Masters, and there were a load of people that were swimming there that I used to swim against. There are other people who swim for the club now who used to be in my old swimming club.

One guy who coached me when I was 16 is now swimming

professionally as a Master in the 55 year old age group. He trains three times a day! He does something like 65,000 metres a week! When I am training I do 15,000 metres!

I joined the club and got an entry form. I had enough confidence now to be able to send entry times in that I was comfortable with.

Now, that was when a second affirmation card was filled out. The first one was the one I mentioned earlier, the second card is a bit more factual, mentioning times I am going to achieve.

I had my stroke sorted, so this was all about speed now. In the last month prior to the championship I trained like a madman! I was just getting quicker and quicker every day!

So we got to the event on the 27/29th October, and I got all my cards back with entry times accepted. My parents had come up from Birmingham as well. They were interested in how I was going to get on, especially since they had lived and breathed it for so many years!

The first event was the 100m breaststroke at 6.30pm on the Friday night. I had taken the day off work, and intended to get there to register by 5.30, otherwise you cannot compete. I thought I would set off from Manchester at 3.00 and get to Sheffield by 5.30.

However, there was a big accident on the motorway.

I could not get across from Manchester to Sheffield without going south to within 20-30 miles north of Birmingham. All the roads across from Manchester were shut because of this accident and all the traffic was being diverted. So I set off at 3.00 and by 5.00 I was still 50 miles away, AND going in the wrong South Westerly direction! I ended up getting there for 6.15! At 5.35, my wife had said that we might as well turn around and go home now, because even if we did get there they wouldn't let me enter.

I said, 'I'm not going to give up! I am going to get there even if I have to watch the event; I am still going to get there!' We got there at 6.15 and I just abandoned the car outside the front porch and said to my dad, 'You park the car. I am going to batter the door down to get into this event!'

So I ran onto the side of the pool and they were warming up, with less than 15 minutes to go. I ran into the officials' office, and said, 'Right I need to register for this event, I know I am late!' I put my ticket down onto the table. He said, 'But you're late.' I explained why.

As luck would have it, one of the early people hadn't turned up.

So they had a couple of slots. He took my ticket and put me in one of the slots. I was in the first heat in lane number three. I got changed, got into the training pool, did a couple of laps, and was ready to start the race.

Now, the deal with these championships is that the age groups run between ages 24 up to age 95 in five year stages.

So you are always going to have a point when you are the youngest and quickest – something to look forward to all the time. Even at age 89!

It is just incredible – you see these guys there who were born in 1911.

So I was in the first heat with the 85-89 year olds! There were all these old guys getting on the starting block and there I was, right in the middle of them!

So, usual stuff – on your marks, get set, go, blasted up and down the pool, and finished first – fortunately! I beat my swimming time and felt pretty comfortable with that.

It was my first event in 20 years and I found myself doing stuff that was automatic when I was 16.

You probably don't realise it but you get into habits when you're a swimmer – your preparation – standing at the end of the block, with the time keeper in front of you and you are watching the race that is going on before yours, and you start doing stuff like wetting your goggles and cleaning them with your fingers. You will keep doing it over and over to get them 100% clear before you put them on your head. I just found myself doing that automatically, not having even remembered doing it before!

It was also the first time I had worn a swimming hat for 20 years. Isn't it weird – I had not trained with a swimming hat, but I had bought one for the event! I just knew I had to wear one to race in – because that was what I used to do. So, I had my swimming hat on, put my goggles on, then polish, polish, polish. And then you start finding yourself shaking out your arms and legs! I remember thinking, 'Hello! I have done this before!'

It was just as if someone had flicked a big switch in my brain and bang, 20 years on I made the same connection again! Autopilot!

I wasn't nervous either! That was the BIG difference between what I did as a junior and what I do now. As a kid I used to get really nervous but last year I thought, 'well, I know what I want to do now, so there's no point getting nervous about it! I feel pretty good about what I'm doing, I can do it, and all the old feelings are coming back!'

The Sunday was the big event for me, the 100 metre freestyle and I really wanted to do the best time I had ever done and when I started training, the time I wanted to see on the ticket was 60 seconds dead.

My goal was just to do what I set out to do, and that was to beat my time and get into the top ten. The 100 metre freestyle came, and I did it - I got into the top ten.

I know I have got a lot quicker and my stroke repetition has come down since October and I reckon I will get under 60 seconds next time I swim and that is the next big goal for me.

That's what it is all about. I reckon I am going to do that easily by probably June. I want to get into an event in June and get under 60 seconds and then have another crack at something like 58 and a bit in Sheffield again this year.

I don't know where I would come in the World Masters, I will worry about that later. I'll see what I can do this year. But top 20 in the World would be pretty good.

By the way, at Sheffield, there was one old guy in the 85-89 age group, who was sitting by the pool minding his own business. He got called up for his event and he had a walking stick. So he picked up his walking stick and hobbled towards the starting block, waiting for his event. He put his goggles on, and polished them, getting ready.

Anyway, he couldn't get on the starting block without help and the time keepers helped him on! I think he was in the 100m breaststroke. He was one of the slower competitors. So he dives in, swims his race and takes a while to complete it! However, he completes his race, gets out of the pool, the time keeper gives him his walking stick and he goes back and hobbles off to his seat and then you find out 10 minutes later that he has broken the World Record for his age group!

It was incredible! There are guys there who are 60-65 who are retired and all they do is swim and they are wearing these big lycra body-suits, the goggles and hats, they have the suntans, they go every day, and they are still doing World Class performances at that time of life. They train three times a day, and keep themselves fit and healthy.

TABLETS OF STONE 3
DESIRE IS THE BEGINNING OF ALL HUMAN ACHIEVEMENT

W CLEMENT STONE

I would never have done any of this before – I mean with everything I have done when it comes to sport in my life, I have never stuck with stuff for long; it has been too difficult and I have given up on it. I wasn't consciously saying that this time it was going to be different, that was not the way I looked at the goal. What I was building was, 'This is the event, this is the time, this is the place, this is the emotion' and everything else just happened around it. So that was the valuable lesson for me.

Too many people think, 'I have to go down to the pool every day', or 'I have to get down to the gym and do this that and the other', and **if you can decouple that**, which is the hard work, **from the end goal, then you will just do it.**

Your point was 'be careful what you wish for because it will come true'. So I achieved what I wanted to do, but then I couldn't get up the next morning!

Mike   *Yes, you lost the drive to go training – because you had achieved your goal.*

Neil   The day after that, I thought, 'well, you're entitled to miss a day. You've achieved what you had wanted, so have a bit of a rest.' I couldn't get up the next day either, or the day after that! It took me about a month and a half to get back into it.

Mike   *Until you set another goal?*

Neil   Effectively, yes. I just couldn't get back into it. Someone had just flicked the switch back off in my head.

Mike   *You had just flicked the switch off! How scary is that!? So what would you say to people who are thinking about coming on the course or who haven't done the course?*

Neil   I have spoken to a lot of people about the course and the general perception is that it is the same old stuff. You know, we have been on this kind of course before, the same old kind of techniques, just a different front on it; **but it's not, it is completely different.**

It's a completely different way of thinking; a completely different way of goal setting.

I had never seen anything like it before. More or less everything that we went through and certainly the first couple of days was just brand new, radical stuff. It focused more on how you think about things, how you think about goal setting, how your brain takes that information and stores it and then unlocks it subconsciously. You do not even have to think about it at the end of the day, it just happens.

You know, you just cannot pick that stuff up anywhere else; I have not seen it anywhere else. Everybody I have spoken to who has been sceptical, by the time they have been on the course, understand the value of it. They have done pretty amazing things. Guys that have smoked since the age of two have stopped!

You can do it; you have the power to do it. Anyone can do it – even children!

My wife struggles with the kids from time to time as most parents do, and part of the message was that you need to reinforce the positives and play down the negatives. It is all too easy when you have kids to say, 'Don't do this, don't do that!'; negative, negative, negative.

I have started using that a lot since the course. My wife Tracey gets really fed up with me for doing it, but it really does work. Thomas came up to me the other night and said, 'I am really terrible at spelling Dad, I cannot spell'. I asked, 'Why is that?' And he said, 'Well, Mummy keeps telling me off when I get words wrong.'

So, I said to Tracey, 'Leave Tom alone for a couple of weeks and let me have a chat about his spelling'. He was getting four or five out of 10 for his weekly test at school. So we had a couple of sessions over a couple of weeks. I tried to reinforce the words he got right and not the ones he got wrong. I just kept going over it. He came back last week and he had got 10 out of 10.

Tracey was amazed. Absolutely gob smacked. She realised that what she was doing at the time felt the right thing to do, telling him that he was getting things wrong and that if he carried on getting stuff wrong he wouldn't be top of the class. She realised eventually that what she was doing was conditioning him to fail. She was pretty terrified.

It really is so simple. Anybody can do it!

It doesn't just work in one slice of life. You can make it work in your home life, your social life.

Typically at work, you have lots of individuals with certain mind-sets and you find that when you go on this course, their brains will still be the same, and it is yours that has changed, and if you are not careful you will end up slipping back into your old habits.

But I found that the success that I have achieved at home and in sport helped me stick with it at work as well.

Mike   *Fantastic, so you are not allowing these people to drag you back down.*

Neil   You find that people start to convert. Almost to the contrary, they make an effort. You are practically hypnotising people.

This is what the course is all about. You have to stick with it. You have to keep talking to them, keep reinforcing the positives and slow down on the negatives. You find that some people who have been sceptics all their lives are turning around!

If you can pull the positive ones in your team with you, then the rest will get the message and follow. That is what I have found. They won't realise that they are doing it.

Even negative people are paranoid about being isolated, so they will jump on board too. That is their game plan - they will jump on board - 'I am isolated, I do not want to be out on a limb, I want to be a part of the team,' you just pull them across.

Mike   *That was fantastic Neil. Thank you.*

RELATE AND ASSIMILATE

Neil is a genuinely nice man, whose achievements in his working and personal lives are outstanding. Despite his achievements, Neil embodies humility and is a terrific leader of his work team.

Neil, you taught me that it is never too late; that we must 'seize the day', and that by being a positive example to those around you, you can massively influence them for the good.

What did Neil teach you?

1

2

3

'IMAGINE IT HAPPENING'

Mike's Introduction

Danielle was on the course with her colleagues from work, and she started day two by holding court to tell us all about an immediate success she had had, not of her own, but in coaching someone she loved. This is an amazing story of a wife, mother, daughter and great team player. Respect, Danielle, respect!

Mike   *So come on Danielle, tell us all about your experience of when you came to i2i, what happened, what did it say to you?*

Danielle The one biggest thing that I got, and I got lots, was the 'can't' thing!

Mike   *I had forgotten about this, I often tell this story at the end of the course, go on.*

Danielle It was just something that you said that just hit me. I think you were talking about running a marathon, and the reason why we can't do it, is because we don't want to enough. But I took that home that night and I said, 'right from now on we do not say "can't", but say "don't want to enough" instead'.

We were watching television, and I just said, 'there is nothing we cannot do if we want to enough'. And of course that was it. Someone said, 'a man can't have a baby', and I said, 'well actually if you really wanted to, a man could adopt a baby and bring it up on his own'. There were all these little things and we sat and discussed them.

Then I said, 'hang on, what if somebody cannot run, if you have no legs', and one of the kids said, 'yes, but you can do a marathon in a wheelchair, if you really, really want to!'

Mike   *How old are the little ones?*

Danielle Robert is 9 and Karen is 11. So we had this discussion, 'we are not going to say "I can't" ', but we are going say "I do not want to enough", and that is perfectly admissible as long as we'll admit that we do not want to do something.

I think that a few weeks later Robert said to my husband Kev, "can you come and watch me play football?" He said "no, no I can't. I've got to go to work". And Robert said, "you don't mean you can't, you mean you don't want to".

Right between the eyes! Kev sat there and he said 'well you are quite right, but if I don't go to work I will get into trouble. Also if I go to work it means that we can go on holiday. We can have a few weeks together if I do overtime,' Kev actually sat and explained it to Robert. At the end of it Robert just said 'OK, see you next week Dad' and he was really happy about it.

Mike   *Because Kev had taken the time to explain?*

Danielle Exactly!

Mike   *How many parents do that?*

Danielle Well, he was forced to explain, he couldn't just say 'can't'. We feel we actually did it this morning with Robert, when he said 'I can't find my coat' and I said, 'what you mean is you do not want to enough and you want me to do it'. 'Yes exactly mum!' We had a little joke about it, but we always say you are not allowed to say the 'c' word, and it is really good!

It is all about making choices and the reasons for making choices and you are mature enough to decide why you are making these choices.

Along those lines, my husband started up a business in December and all throughout our married life, he has wanted to start a business but hasn't, because 'I can't, I haven't got the money' always kicked in. There was always a reason why we couldn't so we basically now said that there is no reason why we cannot.

If you want to do it, you will do it. It was the question, 'do you really want to do it?' that was powerful. The answer, the REAL answer was 'maybe later'. Anyway he set up the business and he is doing ever so well. He is still working at his old job, but he was seeing somebody yesterday and there is a possibility that he will be able to give up work very soon and dedicate himself to his business full time.

With all the problems we have had with it, we have said 'why can't we do this?' and 'what do we have to do in order to do this? 'Well I could do it, but maybe it would mean that I wouldn't go to bed until 2 o'clock in the morning!' The point is simply do we *want* to stay up until 2.00am and do it? **The quality of your thinking is the key!**

Mike   *You are making much better decisions then, aren't you? You are getting to the bottom of something rather than dismissing it. You are really investigating the problem, and communicating.*

Danielle Another thing that you did which I think ties in with this really is not just saying 'you can do whatever you want to do', but rather asking yourself 'what is it that you actually want to do?'

Don't kid yourself - if you say you want to be a millionaire, then do it!

Mike   *That is what most people would say, but most people do not REALLY want that, because of the effort it takes.*

Danielle   Ask instead, 'what really is the personal thing that would give me greatest satisfaction?' and imagine yourself doing it! I think for everybody that I work with, there are not many of them who would say 'I want pots of money in the bank and to have a great time'.

I think that was another thing – if you want to do something then you have to know you *really* want to do it. You have to want to do it enough to make the sacrifices to do it. They may be little sacrifices, but you really have to focus on what you want, and not on what you do not want.

I can happily say now, 'no I am not going to do that because it is not part of the path on my golden plan'. I am not 'lazy', but 'it doesn't mean anything to me, so I am not going to do anything about it'. Honesty, at least!

Mike   *So, you would walk away from that situation in the past and feel quite bad because you have not done something. You are actually saying that you do not feel bad about it because you are choosing not to do it. So don't beat yourself up about it, you are just not doing it. That is positive!*

Danielle   I used to be the world champion at beating myself up - not now though! The first time I came back from one of your review sessions, which are really good, the first time something hit me, it was 'I can't be bothered to do this', and that was something else to beat myself up about! I don't remember what it was now, so it wasn't important, but here I was, recognising this negativity all by myself, and then stopping it, as you taught us to!

I just get myself back on the right path now. It's becoming more and more easy!

Mike   *Do you think it helps working your way through these things?*

Danielle   In two respects; if there are people that you work closely with that you have a great relationship with, then you can support each other.

On the other hand you can approach the people that you do not work so well with, in a different way. If you have a bit of a negative relationship with someone who used to make you think, 'he is going to wind me up today' you can make a different choice. I think that there is a person at work who really has been able to press my button and wind me up without doing anything. I now say to myself, 'I can't wait to see this person this morning because we are going to have a good conversation'. I really believe that, and I have noticed the difference and people at work have noticed the difference. *He* has noticed the difference and it has been really great. Maybe in the beginning it was a bit false, but it isn't now. It has got us through, and has overcome our problems, and it is a good working relationship now. I think it has helped both of us.

Extra feedback and extra encouragement for my family and the people I work with all the time, that's the 'new me'!

Let me remind you of this, too. On the course, we had been for coffee, and we had come back in, and everyone had settled. Just before we started I spoke, telling you that I got home the night before and I was absolutely buzzing. I was like 'hooray!' and the kids were, 'oh my God, where is my mother! Let me speak to MOTHER!' My husband was away, I think he was in Germany, and so I let them have their dinner in the living room, which I would never have done when Kev is home. I was telling them all about the course, 'so if you tell yourself this water is going to be cold, this water is going to be cold and you put your hand in and you feel cold'. I gave them examples like that.

Well, I put the kids to bed that night, and my daughter who would have been seven at the time was having a lot of trouble with bed wetting. I had never ever shouted at her about it because it upset her more than it upset me. She was getting to the age when it was not acceptable for her, and I said, 'try telling yourself that you'll be fine tonight. You'll wake up and just go to the loo if you need to'. I must have done it right! I did not say, 'say I am not going to wee in my bed'. I said the positive and I said to her, 'say 'I am going to get up and go to the toilet', picture yourself in the middle of the night getting up, when you are a little bit cold. Say that to yourself and **imagine it happening.**'

Mike   *What did she say to you when you told her that?*

Danielle She said, 'oh OK mum'. She said she would do it, and so I said 'say it aloud ten times, and then I am going to go down stairs and you're going to say it ten times in your head'. I was really buzzing, so I did not go to bed until about midnight, which was way late for me. About 2 o'clock in the morning I heard 'MUM, MUM! It worked, I have just been to the loo!'

So she came into my bed and she sat there chatting away, and she said, 'I am going to do this all the time', and she has been brilliant ever since! I am not saying she has not had **any** problems, but I must say, she only does it when she is worried about something, but now we just talk it through, and whoosh, it's sorted! What a difference!

Mike   *That is the nice thing about this, at their ages they are already at ease with this 'positivity' thing and they already have the evidence that it works.*

Danielle Well I think that we also use, 'you can do whatever you want in life, you just have to want to do it enough'. We use that all the time and I hope I don't just say it. I say to her about her school work, 'you have to do this for you, I cannot make you do it. I can only tell you what I would like you to do, but you have to make yourself proud, not make me proud and you know what is acceptable'.

Mike   *Tell us about your mum, you e-mailed us some amazing things about her.*

Danielle My mum, it was one of those things that hit me between the eyes. It was just around Christmas. My mum came to stay for a couple of days. I confide in her a lot and she confides in me a lot. She had put on a lot of weight and she always said about me, that I could tell her as it is and so I don't worry about hurting her feelings. I just tell her what I think she should know and not what she wants to hear. I said to her 'mum you have put on a lot of weight and you are looking old'. I'm delicate like that! She said to me, 'I can't lose weight, I have tried, I can't lose weight', and I actually sat her down and said, 'look, you can do whatever you want to do in life'.

I told her about you and all the positive thinking and what she is telling herself. She is telling herself that she cannot lose weight and so she can't, and so that is a self fulfilling prophecy. I said 'mum just you think what you have done in life'. It was only when I actually said that, I thought back to when I was eight. I am the middle of three children; my sister was ten and my baby brother was three weeks old when my dad committed suicide. He had been ill for some time, but it was out of the blue. He had seemed very happy, up and bright, so it was a big shock for everyone.

My mum had never been out to work. She had part time jobs in shops and things like this. We had no insurance money because dad had committed suicide and we had no money in the bank.

64

She had three kids one of whom was three weeks old! Where do you go from there?

I said to her, 'you look back and imagine saying to yourself that in twenty years' time you are going to have three children who are either married or in stable relationships, they all have good jobs and none of them have ever been in trouble with the police, done drugs or alcohol, and you have a great job, you are doing exactly what you had always wanted to do, you have a lovely little flat, almost a brand new little car, go on holiday twice a year. How would you have said you would do that?'

She said, 'I would have said I couldn't do it and that there was no way I could do it'.

'What made you do it?' I asked. She said, 'you lot - you were the most important things for me, I had to bring you up the way I wanted to bring you up. I had no choice, I had to go and get a job. No other choice.'

We moved because my mum didn't want to be where people knew us and knew our circumstances. We moved to a different house, after my brother got to about six months old and she went out and got a job and worked all the hours God sent. The three of us would drag ourselves up, but she was always very solid for us and always there for us mentally. She had a real strict code of behaviour and what was acceptable and what was not.

She was really strong with all three of us. She did it, and it wasn't, 'why am I doing this?', but rather 'I have to do it'. We went through it and discussed it and I said 'you can lose two bloody stones if you want to!' I went to see her yesterday and she really has lost weight and she said 'I am so happy'. I said 'you are looking really great' and she said, 'well thanks, it means a lot to me and I feel great'.

She is retiring soon, so again like when we grew up, her actual work is finally coming to an end, and perhaps she thought 'I am not as useful as I used to be'.

It was really a case of what do you want to do? What do you need to do? What is important to you? She is really focused and she is a really strong person, and one of the things in life that I have always done is said 'well if my mother can do that, I can do it', and so now I get up and have a go at it. She used to work ten hour days and get the bus home with all the shopping, and I think now when I go home and I moan that I have had a hard week, it is nothing. Then when she was about 45 or a bit younger, she had done well in Marks and Spencer. She was a supervisor and things were becoming a lot easier for her. She had her own income coming in, and a couple of the kids were off her hands. She decided that was not what she wanted to do with her life. She had always wanted to work with mentally handicapped people. She resigned and went as a volunteer to start with, then she got a job, and now she is the manager of the home. She has a fantastic career now. Most people in their lives will never face a situation like she has. Most of us will never face that and yet we moan about the little things that we've got to cope with.

I think a lot of these stories you hear about how people have got through great personal tragedies, or injury, are a little bit enlightening, and you do celebrate the human spirit. But beyond that, it is important to reflect on what the worst that can happen to you is, and how you would get through it, and what you would use to get through it, and why you would get through it.

A lot of people have specific goals, 'I am going to get through it because of...' In my mum's case, we, her children, were her reason. You hear about the people who lost a leg and who say 'I am going to walk because I am going to walk my daughter up the aisle.' I think that perhaps what I have had to do is focus on why I am going to get over these tiny little problems that I have to face.

But when something becomes a major problem, focus on those important things, your reasons to win.

Mike   *Has the course helped you find focus on your reasons more than you used to before?*

Danielle Yes. I did things before by thinking 'what' I should do, and 'how' to do it - exams, work, whatever - but never 'why' I should do it. And yes, you made me aware of that. 'Why should I?' is a powerful question, isn't it?

Mike   *That in itself is fantastic, we usually spend too little time focusing on the 'why', we focus on the 'how', but of course the 'how' is not so important. To find the 'how', you focus on the 'why'.*

Danielle I think that if nothing else is clear, your mind subconsciously allows your brain to work on its own, without you putting all sorts of baggage and issues in its way. Now, I say, 'this is what I am going to do', 'this is what I want', 'this means something to me. I am not sure how I am going to achieve it, just relax and let it come'. Nine times out of ten, it comes to you. You said it was like magic, Mike, and it is, it really is!

Danielle's Story

"We are not going to say 'I cant'!!!"

RELATE AND ASSIMILATE

Were you expecting a story like that? I love this one, because with Danielle's story, you get a mother, wife, daughter, ambitious achiever, and committed employee all rolled into one, so many perspectives on what the power of 'positivity' really means.

Isn't truth truly stranger than fiction! I hope she inspired you to put up with your lot and stay positive, in all aspects of your life.

She most certainly inspired me.

Write below what three lessons Danielle's story has taught you :)

1

2

3

MIRACLE GRO

Mike's Introduction

Martin is Head of Wellfield High School, and a top man, who plays golf with his father Peter, and his son, Dan, at Royal Birkdale. Martin brought us in to help him at school, no, not with his sums, but with a year ten group. The results? Spectacular, but I'll let him tell you.

Mike   *Tell us how we came to be involved with you?*

Martin   I can be very clear sighted about this now, because two things came together.

One was that I had, in my early days of teaching, taught Andrew O'Donoghue, your colleague, and he obviously remembered me with some affection, rather than a sudden fear as we sometimes remember our teachers with!

Secondly, Gillian Ashurst, who worked with you and also worked with me, has experienced your work in the football field, inspiring her son and his friends in a young lad's football team project you ran for Lancashire Constabulary. She said we should meet because we would get on well together and have a lot in common. That proved to be the case.

We got together and we talked about what we might do. We found it very easy to get ideas from that and found that experiencing the course was a prerequisite for you in terms of our relationship and a prerequisite for us as teachers. You had to do it to us first, before we let you do it to our kids!

You then arranged for me and some of my staff to come on a course and it was an interesting experience, especially in the sacred school holidays. There were about five or six of us who started off and three of us who finished. I would say that that was not a sign that it wasn't a success for everybody, I would say it was a sign that it is not an easy process, and a lot of it depends on where you are as a person, as well as where the course will take you.

Some of my team couldn't or weren't ready to look that deeply into themselves and to change what they were doing or re-evaluate what they were doing or reassess what they were doing. I think others were, and I think that for those of us who went through it, the benefit has been long lasting.

Mike   *How did you feel afterwards?*

Martin	Inspired would be the number one, enthused would be another word, and keen to get on with it.
Mike	*For yourself or for the kids?*
Martin	I would say for myself mostly, but I would see the two as fairly inseparable; you can't split them up really because as a teacher what you do has a direct effect on the kids.

I accept that for me, in a fun sort of way, some of the targets set were very personal and were to do with leisure time activities and they have proved equally effective.

I play golf, and golf must be 90% in your head and 10% in your body. People who have problems with golf find it's mostly up in the head. I had this little problem that no matter where I played I would stand on the first tee and make a complete hash of my first shot - it was definitely in my head!

If anyone was watching I couldn't do it; if it's the first tee I couldn't do it. Get that out of the way, on the second tee I was fine; third tee fine; but the first tee - I'd think 'I'm not going to hit it; I'm going to make a mess of it!'

So, one of the targets I set myself was that I would have this clear picture; that I would see the ball disappearing down the fairway and it would be a lovely sunny day – right down the middle; and it works! Just in a silly way it works, because the picture was clear, it was quite clear what I was going to do and I did work on it and I did keep revisiting it. I may have the occasional bad shot off the first tee like anybody will, but 99% of the time it is not a problem.

Little things like that have been good for me and I think being a Head Teacher is a lonely job and you need feeding, like a plant, we need 'Miracle Gro', one of the things that one of our kids said when we did the course; you asked, 'how do you make a tree recover and grow?', and Craig shouted, 'stick some Miracle Gro on it!' Priceless!

So, you do, you need regenerating and when you are the head of a school, obviously you talk to people; you talk to lots of people all day, but you don't usually talk to people who are doing the same job as you, and you are expected, like any leader of an organisation, to be positive. You are expected to be great whatever happens. The course was of great benefit to me, just expanding on the theory of being positive, having some techniques which I could go back to when things get tough; because they do get tough, for everybody.

Mike	Did you set some goals for the school?
Martin	I did, and they have been achieved and new ones are in place now. The group I taught were varied. The group set goals for grades, and they got them; and they were not unambitious grades, but they were a low ability group. To get them actually to turn up for the exam was an achievement! And they did, and they got their grades and they got a sense of pride out of that.

We needed a retractable seating unit in the school. We had had this old unit for about 20 odd years and it was broken and dilapidated and a pain to sit on, a pain to use and . . .

Mike	Whereabouts was this?
Martin	This was in the school theatre and it was an important piece of equipment for the school, because when anybody comes for an event they sit on it and it was horrible to sit on! We knew the local authority wouldn't find the money for us, and we knew we would have to find the majority of the money ourselves.

So we set our stall out to do that and we raised £12,000 and we got the seating unit and I think the 'ID' said that I would be 'sitting on this seating unit on June 1st' - and I was! 'It is June 1st and I am sitting on this seating unit' and I was! So it works, it does work, and I am convinced, utterly convinced that as teachers if we can get better at setting targets and more importantly getting our pupils to set targets we would make enormous strides forward and that is irrespective of what subject they do.

Mike	*I'm convinced that **everybody** does set goals but they just don't realise that they do it. They then subconsciously move towards these goals that they don't know they're setting; they just have no idea they are doing it!*
Martin	I think most people know what their goals are, and yes they are in the back of the head somewhere, but I think they don't set precise goals; it's not in our culture; it's not in our education system, and it should be! If people have the ability to set exact targets then they will achieve them and we have proved that, and **you** have proved that in so many different walks of life. Where we have used this in school, and we have only scraped the surface of that, it is working, there is no doubt about it, but we must improve in the ability to set targets.
Mike	*You gave us the pleasure of working with that group of youngsters and it was enjoyable from our point of view as*

well, to experience their achievement in being positive. You gave them leadership, and set the goals, and they had no problem with the techniques at all, not from my perspective they didn't.

Martin   That's the frustrating thing about it; it isn't difficult to learn how to do it! It sticks with you, providing you keep regenerating it, and refreshing it, and going back to it.

Left to your own devices, like any human being, the hurly burly of your day and your work and your life, you can forget. Putting off those things you think will wait is the problem. You've got to go and have this meeting with this person, or the teacher's typical thing is, 'I've got to teach the syllabus; if I don't get through the syllabus, they won't pass their GCSE exams'. It doesn't make a blind bit of difference if they are not interested does it? If they're not interested in what they are doing, and they don't see the point in it, and they haven't set a target for what they are going to do; you can do as many syllabuses as you like, it won't help them! It will just be boring, irrelevant and a waste of time and money! So schools need to be doing this - first of all with teachers on a wide spread basis. They need to be doing it at primary school level. It's like anything, you cannot start early enough. We put off the wrong things.

Mike   *It's a habit isn't it?*

Martin   Yes, and we've proved, working with kids, the earlier the better; it's not an intellectual issue.

Mike   *Absolutely not.*

Martin   They are probably more open minded and therefore more receptive and they can teach us a lot.

Mike   *Coming on to that, the response that we got from this group of young people was amazing; they took us in didn't they, and we felt part of the school, and we felt part of their lives for a year.*

Martin   The way we did it was to make it extraordinary for them and in some ways special. The kids we worked with were not easy, they were our most difficult kids; there were some unstable kids; there were some with the most complex home backgrounds. They were kids who if you'd written it down at the beginning of the course, 75% of them would have failed and/or not got anything out of the education system.

They didn't fail, and they did get something out of the system, and part of what they have gained is incalculable; but I think it will come back to them and it is part of their thinking now and their memory and their life.

So that is no small achievement and I think one of the things we did learn is that we had to actually take the school out of it in order to get them to come to it fresh. It had to be different from school, and that is sad in a way, but it was common sense really that they didn't want more of the same, they wanted something different.

That is something that perhaps we have to learn from the experience; it has got to be different and the difference was important. They have enough, five or six lessons a day, five days a week, it had to be different; the venue had to be different; the presentation had to be different, and that made it more memorable.

Mike   *From your point of view in terms of what they achieved, how do you summarise that?*

Martin   We already said what the kids were like. What did they achieve? First of all, they stayed in school which is no insignificant achievement, because truancy and attendance and keeping kids in school has become a big problem and will become a bigger problem. So number one, to keep them at school was success in itself. Second, they turned up and sat their exams. Actually sitting the exams is almost as important as passing them.

Mike   *Why do you say that?*

Martin   Because often, those kids get to that stage of the year 11 exams, and they think, 'to hell with it, I'm not going to do very well in this, so what is the point? I am not going to do anything with these qualifications; I don't value them; what is the point – I'm not turning up!' They are frightened of the failure, but then again they have had that failure maybe reinforced, so why turn up for some more?

So the 19 of them came and sat those exams and they did them ALL, all 167 exams, and they all ended up with grades and some of them with better grades than they expected to get. They really appreciate that, in that they'd done it, and got proof that's on a piece of paper that said 'certificate'; and some of them who would go nowhere near a Presentation Ceremony in the evening, came and were proud of what they had achieved, so that was very important. Amazing!

The third thing that we achieved was that they all, with perhaps one exception, have gone on to do something, because that is the group of kids who in the past would be 'floaters'; would be non-committal, unemployed, wandering around with nothing to do, getting into trouble, negatively impacting their community.

I'm not saying they're all angels; I'm not saying they're all totally law abiding citizens, but we know from tracking them that they either went in to training or further education or into employment, and a lot of that was down to the target setting work that we did with them, about seeing the bigger picture!

It was, not just 'what are you going to do in a year's time?' It was, 'what are you going to do in five years' time or ten years' time?' and I don't think any people had sat down with them and actually had that discussion with them, a dialogue that asked, 'have you thought how are you going to get there', and 'what is that going to look like?' and 'what is that going to mean?' That's important, so it was a success.

Undoubtedly they felt better about themselves! Did they feel special? Yes, and again that was something those kids hadn't had! We only gave them four or five 'injections' if you like and it was a significant amount of time, but compared to the total amount of time of education they got, it was a small drop. Imagine what more could be achieved if it was done every week? Instead of tutorials at school we have 'positive thinking' now!

Mike   *That was one of the things that you did well, that we were aware of. Although it may have been a month or six weeks in between us seeing them, we knew that you were there keeping it going, weren't you?*

Martin   I think that if this is to take off on a wider scale, that's part of the model that you have got to build; somebody who is on board with it, in sync with it, reminding them..

Mike   *You were using it in assemblies, and you told me you came back from school trips where kids were using some of the language to each other!*

Martin   I used it with my football team and there is a lad in the football team who knocked on my door this weekend and he said he had got something and it was a lovely page from a book he had found.

Mike   *Are you going to read it?*

Martin   He found this and I said it is a bit like that advertisement that they have for the Post Office, the 'I saw this and I thought of you' thing. And that's what he said 'I saw this and thought of you'! It's headed 'Think Positive' followed by a little poem:

Think Positive
Only if you think you can't, you'll find you really won't
Only if you think negative, that voice will tell you don't
We are all faced with life decisions, some maybe big, some small
But unless you're thinking positive, you'll never make any at all.
So the answer's very simple; think things over, think them through
Believe in yourself completely and the answer's there for you!

Mike   *That's beautiful! It's great that he thinks of you in that way.*

Martin   I was really happy and another lovely thing, one of the little kids said 'we use that phrase in school all the time, **"if you think you can, you can, and if you think you can't, you're right"**', and one boy, who had only been in the school a few weeks, asked someone else 'Who thought of that phrase?' and he answered 'Mr Ainsworth'! (We think it came from Mark Twain, but it was really nice that he thought, 'well that's really Mr Ainsworth!')   It's nice that when he sees Mr Ainsworth, he thinks positively.

When you are a Head Teacher a lot of the time you are telling kids off and dealing with kids' problems and it is really important that there has to be a balance of that – positive as well as negative.

The course has helped me keep positive and keep going back to that and it's not necessarily just the course, it's being with other people who have been on the course or who are like minded. The meetings that we have had on a regular basis have to reinforce things. To go back and be with other positive people who believe in that ideal and moving that forward, is really important. You come away from those meetings feeling energised.

Mike   *If you were speaking to a young person or even a parent who you thought could benefit, what would you tell them about this? Why would you encourage them to do it?*

Martin   I would encourage them to do it, because it works but only if and when they are ready. They have got to want to do it.

Mike   *Because it's not easy?*

Martin	Exactly, because it's not a soft ride; it's not just sitting there and you've got to actually take part in it, and different people are in different situations, so you would have to perceive who would really benefit and who would really need it. I mean everybody will benefit from it, but it's timing – when's the best time and place, and opportunity to do that.
Mike	*What would you say they would get out of it?*
Martin	They would get direction – that is number one, and I do believe that a lot of us let life do it to us, rather than us controlling our lives. 'I had no choice' 'I had no control' 'it's just happening to me' and 'it's coming at me in waves'.

What the course does is to let you get the chance to rise above that and have a good look from the helicopter at what's going on and just take stock. Again we're not good at that, we're not good at that in education, just standing back, we tend to just grind on and on and on, very task orientated. Everybody wants to do well, but sometimes you have got to think, 'could I do this differently?' I just think we are obsessed with content in education, obsessed with it and at the end of the day it is the person that matters – if you don't have their heart, you don't have their soul or their mind, so it doesn't matter!

Good communication, and someone who makes you feel special is crucial and that's one of the things that we did with those kids. They may not be able to put it into words but I know that they felt special and a lot of the time they don't feel special. They feel their self esteem is very low and they are unhappy; perhaps without the emotional framework to be able to put that in to words, but they are unhappy and frustrated and what we did, and what you're very good at, and what Andrew's very good at - making people feel special.

Mike	*But parents could help you so much couldn't they? As a parent I could do so much more, and of course, most do.*
Martin	Absolutely and we could do so much together; what have we got in common? We have the child, of course. When it goes wrong, it's often because we're at odds with one another, and when it goes right it's because we are all singing from the same hymn sheet. We want to get involved together but it happens very little.
Mike	*You could really make it fun too.*
Martin	You can bring in all these home/school agreements which says

'the school would do this, and the pupils would do this, the family would do this', but that's just a bit of paper at the end of the day; but a positive thinking course would be much more powerful, getting them all to come and getting them all together. At the end of the day if it was good; if the product was good, and the experience was good, and the parents could see it was doing them good, and their kids good, it would just put things on a completely different footing than the way they are now. There are huge possibilities for you in education, Mike, and what you are doing is education at the end of the day, in any shape or form, but will people take it up? Will Governors or Teachers change their ways? They need to!

Mike   *And what else are you up to?*

Martin   The 'IDs' are going well; there was the golfing one and there were three or four to do with school, the ones I set the first time through are all finished and complete, and we are on to the next lot. I have been working in school on target setting, and we are not quite there yet, because we have just not trained ourselves as to how to do it, and how to write a good 'Inevitable Dream', and if we are going to go further with that, we have got to spend some time actually training the staff to do that, and then they can train other people to do it.

So it's the usual thing until they can actually touch it they won't believe it! I'm sure I read a story about that once.

RELATE AND ASSIMILATE

What about those kids! All of them, with possibly one exception, 'engaged' in something useful, and with 167 GCSE Certificates between them.

I attended the Presentation Night, spoke at it actually, and it was fantastic to experience the pride of 'The Wellfield Winners', aka 'The Invincibles' in their achievements.

Martin is an inspirational leader, and keeps standards of attitude and expectation high.

Being and staying positive is a daily discipline, and he understands that and is prepared to show leadership by setting a personal example.

I loved how he said we made the children feel 'special', because that is something we can all do.

Who do you know who needs to be made to feel special today?

Got your 'Miracle Gro'? (Thanks to Scotts, by the way for allowing Andrew to reference their awesome 'Miracle Gro' product - buy some!)

Well, what are you waiting for?

Go get 'em!

So what did Martin teach you?

1

2

3

'THE RACE IS LONG, AND IN THE END, IT'S ONLY WITH YOURSELF'

Mike's Introduction

This story doesn't need one, just strap yourself in, and hang on if you can!

Mike   So John you came on the i2i course and I looked at you and knew you would fly with what I was going to teach you. I get a feeling about people, and I knew about you. So tell us where were you and what did it do to you?

John   I was pretty driven, always had been since I'd had a major setback, where I failed University; didn't get my degree and I'd always felt that I had wasted those two years in terms of making progress. I always felt that there were two years there wasted to never get back.

Mike   *You let yourself down?*

John   Yes, so I have spent a lot of years since then trying to catch up/ claw back that time. I'm not one of these people now that can comfortably sit and do nothing for a day; I have to do something every day; move myself forward to the point of excess really, and it is something that has always bothered me. I could never just relax on a Sunday afternoon in the pub with my mates. I always wanted to do something to help claw back these two years. I'd just got promoted to Sergeant after being demoted from transferring forces so I had that to deal with as well.

Mike   *Which force were you in before?*

John   I was in West Midlands, transferred up to here, and had to take a drop to PC, so another two years wasted - so I was thinking 'I've got to catch up - catch up!'

I'm always busy, but I was so busy I never got to bed early! I really did struggle with that because I could never get out of bed. I was tired no more than anyone else but used to get patches of not depression, but patches of being fed-up; patches of it being an effort; but outwardly I was reasonably successful.

I'd already built and moved in to a house when I was 24; I found a plot of land when I was 22, and when I came to you I'd already paid the mortgage off. I was looking to buy another plot of land to build a second house. I was successful in my own small way, but I had demons and I was unfulfilled.

I went on the course after spending years of reading about positive thinking; I read all these popular psychology books and tossed them aside. I took pieces on board, the odd phrase, the odd saying, but the two days on the course were like a light being turned on.

I loved the way it was put together; why you think the way you think. For the first time I was learning about the power of the subconscious, and I suppose in addition to that it got me thinking about what I could do; my potential and how I'd wasted a lot of my time. So I started just reflecting.

I've only ever been able to take on one project at a time and I will work on that to the exclusivity of everything else until it's done. Then I move on to the next thing. Now I'm a lot more balanced and I've got four or five projects on at any one time and I can do them all and switch off and move on to the next one over a period of several days!

The second main difference is that I'm now motivated. Before I was merely clawing back time, achieving as much as I could to get back the time I'd wasted at university and the time I'd spent getting demoted and coming back and messing around making up for this disorganised life that I had led. Now I've done it because I'm motivated just to do what I want to do; set myself goals because I want to achieve them.

I know now that I'm not going to die until I decide to die; OK I might get hit by a bus but the chances are I won't. I'm probably going to live until I'm 95 or 100 and if they crack cancer, heart disease and Alzheimer's in the next 30 or 40 years I could anticipate living until I'm 100 or 120!

That's how I'm living my life now, because I believe that I'm in no rush; so it's banished my demons and I'm not rushing around anymore.

I'm not particularly talented in any specific area, but the quality I do have is my capacity for work. I can outwork anybody - even motivated people - so yes I'd never get anywhere on natural ability, but I'm prepared to outwork people and the course gave me the mental capacity to grind the results out.

Look at the Police Inspectors Exam. I sat down for six months and ground it out – there was no way I was going to fail that exam. I sat down, got four questions wrong out of 65 and I knew that I'd got 61 right and I came home and said to my family, 'I've passed that'.

I know other people have not revised and have taken the exam two or three times and in the end wasted two years, so what I got from you was the *capacity* to take that exam.

It gave me the capacity to take on this house where every day I achieved hardly anything – so I ground it out and 15 months later the house is a palace and it's done. The point is that **you might not achieve much every day but you achieve *something* every day.**

I do something towards each of my goals every day. That means every year I have 365 actions in respect of each goal and so I've had three years and over 1,000 actions with respect to each goal!

Mike   *How many people could do that?*

John   Everybody! Sometimes all I do, if I'm busy is sit there stretching so that I'm supple when I start training. We might be going out for dinner and I won't have time for a full run, so instead I'll nip for a 20 minute run. In that way the next time I train I've retained some of my fitness. It may only be 20 minutes, but I've achieved something towards my goal, and that's all I do now; I make sure I achieve something.

Some days I achieve much more than others but every day I do something. That's a major difference in my life.

Balance is important too. I balance my hobbies, I balance work and I balance my home life equally so that I no longer do things to the exclusion of all else because that would be destructive. Whilst you achieve in one area, you could be neglecting everything else; your relationships can suffer, your work can suffer, hobbies suffer. Now they are completely balanced I can go to bed every night knowing I've done something towards each one. It's nice and balanced so no one is missing out now. I've been a lot happier because I'm no longer feeling guilty about the things I'm neglecting.

Mike   *I think you are right John, a lot of people would put a lot of energy into the work and there is almost no energy left for anything else.*

John   That's the trouble, but when you have the right frame of mind which I now have, you've got enough energy to do them all. If you do it right, you have enough energy to do them all because when you have done a good job at work you come home and you're fresh. I come home with more energy now than when I go to work!

I get up in a morning and I'm awake. I go and get my boys and we have 20 minutes watching television, singing and laughing and it's great!

Mike   *I remember you commenting on that.*

John   And another thing I learned; when you walk in to a room full of people you haven't met before, don't think 'oh they're not going to like me', or 'I don't like any of these people'; pinch yourself and say **'these are the friends I've not met yet'.** You said it as a joke Mike, but it's so right!

Now I walk into a room and I don't worry that people might think I'm a little jumpy or un-cool, or a little bit full of energy. I don't care even in the police environment when it's frowned upon, and there are some people looking a bit sideways. I don't give a damn; I'm me, get on with me!

I aim to never make an enemy now. No more confrontations in the car shouting at people who have cut me up; none of that. It took me a long time to overcome it and what I will say is that when you haven't seen the light you get satisfaction from shouting at people and telling them off, but then you're the one wound up for half an hour and it's dangerous wasted energy. Forget it; let it go; let them cut you up and drive off; sit there smiling to yourself because it is not worth the effort.

I know someone at the moment who likes horses and she's always hitting the tops of cars with her riding crop - having confrontations with drivers. I go for a walk and I see she's rung the police again complaining about yet another driver; but what is she getting out of it?

She's getting herself all wound up, she's getting angry, she's having confrontations, and she's going to end up getting hurt, because road rage is now fashionable; it's now acceptable in society - she'll end up getting hurt and will get nothing out of it apart from the satisfaction of telling the police! I just write it off now and let it go. I come home in a good mood - and what a difference!

I'd like to say this - if anyone has got a personality like mine which is inherently confrontational, doesn't like backing down, or giving way, just give way - it isn't worth the energy to spend on confrontation - lose the battle and win the war.

I also always used to judge my success or my happiness in relation to other people - relatives etc. Now I've removed myself from that. I'm no longer bothered about what anyone else is doing because they've all got different goals; all got different backgrounds. Now I'm only worried about what I'm doing and another demon has gone. **I'm not competing with anyone.**

If six people want me to fail, why should I focus on those six people? I forget about it now. When I go in a room and it's full of people I don't know, I'm me; and if six of those twenty people decide not to like me I don't care because now I know fourteen of them will be my friends, which would not have happened before.

In the past, I would have ended up speaking to one or two people and being quite critical of the others. Now the difference in attitude and the difference in response that you get from people for being open, friendly and showing your weaknesses is amazing!

I don't even try to be cool anymore because I've got too much energy to be cool. I can't sit there and be slow; I'm all over the place. I'm not the most popular person in the world but people warm to me more now.

Two other significant things, working with you makes you analyse what you want in life. I had goals, but I didn't really analyse why I wanted this or why I wanted that. There are some things that I did want before, that I'm not bothered about; I wanted them for the wrong reasons, don't need them – you realise after the course that you've got the time to sit down and think about what you actually want. Sometimes in winter, with the dark nights when there is nothing going on, I go for an hour's fast walk because the endorphins released from that give me a good feeling. I don't talk about it. If anyone says to me 'what are you going to do tonight?' I don't say to them "I'm going to go for a walk". But I go for an hour's walk and enjoy it; I never seem to feel low. Since the course I feel happier.

Two days with you didn't solve that, but gave me the know-how to think 'how can I ensure I don't get depressed anymore? I can do something about this, go to bed a bit earlier get myself organised, take St John's Wort' – so I also obtained the tools to go and find out what's wrong. The course didn't solve anything really, but **showed me I had to go out and find the answers for myself.**

One of the things that I was confused with at first was that I thought I would now be 100% happy and if I encapsulated all the principles you taught me and adopted them and utilised them that I would be happy all the time. It isn't quite like that however; being successful sometimes is about allowing yourself to experience disappointments; to feel, **'Inspirational Dissatisfaction'** you call it Mike, so that you analyse it, know that you don't want to feel it again, and it gives you the motivation to go on.

When I look at people like Richard Branson, they're not happy all the time, but they have a positive philosophy that enables them to deal with disappointment, deal with failure, enables them to deal with areas that they don't like by doing something about it.

So these people that are 100% positive that have been through this, the Mike Finnigans, they're not 100% happy all the time.

They just know how to get through life and do what they want to do and deal with other things.

I know what you are teaching is to live a fulfilled life and to be happy overall but to get there you've got to grind things out.

Studying for an exam is boring but you are not going to get that feeling of satisfaction until you put the work in, the effort in, and the effort isn't what you teach, but when you've been through your programme, you realise you've got to grind results, you've got to get down and just get the work done. That isn't enjoyable, but afterwards it's worth it.

And the reason it's worth it for me is because now I'm not sitting around taking statements, going through all the dull jobs.

I'm the one now that plays the strategic role and does what I joined the police to do, to **make a difference**; to make an impact on the community, on society, and that's what I'm able to do now, because I've put in the work and ground out the results.

It wasn't enjoyable, but essential. At first I missed the point. Initially I thought the course would make me happy all the time without having to put the effort in but that's just not the case. You have to put the effort in and you have given me the *courage* to put the effort in.

Mike   *You're right, the guy who does Riverdance, Michael Flatley, says (one of his major quotes) "All of us get pain in life; you can either have it now or you can have it later, I'm taking mine now". He's working to have no regrets, so he'll have the pain now. I saw a slogan the other day that said, 'Pain Pays', and it's right.*

John Well, my mortgage will be paid off again in two years and I am not going to have to use my pension and my commutation to pay it off. I drive an old car but we won't owe a penny in two years; everything will be paid for and then we can just live our lives. I'm only in my thirties, I'll have paid it all off and be in the house of my dreams, all paid for and decorated, gutted throughout and we've had the pain now and now we can have 80 years of pleasure after 10 years of pain. There are going to be no pensions for us unless we pay for them ourselves; we can't rely on a state pension. So all these people who are having it all now will end up with a lot of pain unless they do something about it. It's never too late!

Mike *Another quote says - **Most people sacrifice what they want most for what they want now.***

John How many Olympic champions end up sitting in pubs with their friends on a Saturday night? I mean **potential** Olympic champions - because instead of going training they want to be out there with their mates? For six months I didn't do anything for myself except study and it paid off unbelievably.

Mike *But the point of looking back at it is - the pain is gone.*

John Yes, I don't think about it anymore. When I think about the whole six months of that studying - four hours a day - I have hardly any memory of it.

Mike *Yes, yet the memory of the achievement is there forever.*

John If I get no further now I've satisfied myself. The most phenomenal - you can't put this in your book; it's a secret that no one knows about until they've been on the course - the most phenomenal thing ever in my life was understanding the power of the subconscious mind. I've never ever been able to relate that to anyone properly because I get so excited!

If you believe it, you can do it. The way you guys explain that is unbelievable and that's what I never picked up in ten years of reading all these books. I never picked that up, because you managed to put together something that made it believable, so now I can do anything now, absolutely anything.

Mike *Yes, and you always could.*

John Yes, you wouldn't believe the projects I'm doing now. I'll give you another example of why you have indirectly helped. Without the programme I wouldn't have read books about people that I admire. For example I wouldn't have read Richard Branson's autobiography, so I wouldn't have realised just how limitless the possibilities are. When you read you realise that he's not hemmed in by anything. He started his own airline because he was stuck in an airport so he rang someone and asked about chartering a plane didn't he? He chartered a plane and sold tickets and that was the start of Virgin Airlines!

This year, I'm going to buy a little terraced house in Blackpool and rent it out. Then when I've proved myself to the bank, I'm going to get a ten year business development loan, and then I'll buy six houses and then I might do it again.

The point is I'm not going to limit myself by just buying one or two and I've had a check with a financial advisor and once you've got one up and running and it's paying for itself, you can get the others. I could easily end up with two dozen, and I'm not bothered about making any money out of each of them. I just want them to pay for themselves, pay the mortgage over the months and in ten years I might own 24 houses outright.

So with an initial outlay of £3,000 for the deposit on my first one, in ten years I could be selling 24 houses that have been completely paid for!

All of a sudden, the point is, I'm alert to the possibilities and that is what I'm going to do. It is simple and it won't even cost me anything and even if it's a risk it's unbelievable!

Mike   *Isn't it amazing John, that what you are saying here is that you actually had the ability and the talent all the time to do that?*

John   I encountered your course at 30; if I'd have encountered it at 18 you wouldn't believe the difference. I would not be sitting here now. I would just have got so much further. My sons though will have the principles from day one. If my parents had given me the principles, the positive thinking principles that I have now got; if I'd learned the social skills that I've now learned that were triggered from going on the course; if I knew the limitless possibilities and the fact that your background doesn't make a bit of difference; then at 18 I'd have gone so much further it would be unbelievable!

I limited myself; I limited my ambitions until I was 30 and they only became unlimited after I went on the course. OK so it's not too late - but don't leave it till you retire to go on one of your courses - do it now!

Mike	*Imagine yourself John ten years from now, you'll be in your forties - imagine what you can accomplish in ten years. It will be fantastic!*
John	I appreciate that, but the point is don't put it off, do it now. Things change from day one. The week after the programme, I'd done so many more things; I got fitter, I slept better, I had a plan - knew exactly what I wanted, where I was going in my life, all in a week. I'd made more progress in the seven days from going on the course than in the previous 13 years even though outwardly perhaps it looked like I'd achieved a lot!
Mike	*I remember you saying to me fairly early on 'I found an extra couple of hours in every day that I didn't know were available'.*
John	Absolutely unbelievable. I'm still the best person in the world for wasting time even now - I can still waste two hours a day easily.
	If I'm left to my own devices I can spend two hours having my breakfast and having a wash!
Mike	*Are you still doing your running?*
John	I always used to say I want the 100 metres, that's the glamour one. I want to get that buzz from running as fast as I can and winning a race. You look at a runner after a 100 metres race slowing himself down and it's a good feeling. I always had in the back of my mind that I wanted to be a 100 metres runner, but everyone always discouraged me.
	I went on the course and thought, 'right what do I want to do?' I'd always kept myself fit, so I got my garage decked out as a gym, saved myself half an hour travelling time to the gym, saved myself £300 a year every year by not paying for a gym and saved myself plenty of time.
	So I came out of the course and thought 'although I'm 31 I'm going to start doing 100 metres'. I turned up one night at Stanley Park athletics track and I stood there and watched everybody and there was a group sprint training. I walked over and said 'I'm John, I've not done 100 metres since I was at University and even then it was only 12.1. I'm 31 now and I wondered if I could start training with you and perhaps get a couple of races?' I expected that they wouldn't look at me twice until I'd proven my commitment but no, they welcomed me with open arms - come and join us - 4 × 200 metres and 4 × 100 metres that night, I did the first 4 × 200 metres and I had to sit down because I knew I was going to be sick!

Anyway I spent the next three or four months training and really getting myself fit. It took four months before I could do a full training session with them! These people are on the verge of the British team and I didn't realise that at the time. They've had 10 years of 12 or 13 sessions a week behind them, so that's the standard they are at. It took me three or four months before I could complete a full session. But I can do a full session now AND I ran three races last year. I came last in two of them!

TABLETS OF STONE 4
LEARN AND USE THE THREE KEY VITAL ELEMENTS OF MY SUCCESS SYSTEM THAT NEVER FAILS — KNOW WHAT YOU WANT; KNOW WHY YOU WANT IT; AND KEEP WORKING UNTIL YOU FIND OUT HOW TO GET IT

W CLEMENT STONE

Mike   *And for twenty years you missed out on that because?*

John   Because I limited myself.

Mike   *And allowed other people to limit you!*

John   Yes and the important thing is I've not said, 'well I've missed out on 13 years so it's too late now'. I didn't say that, and that is what the tendency is. What I said was, 'I'm going to do it', and I will get satisfaction, and my target is to go first across that finish line and get that same feeling that they have.

In the last three years it's mounted up to promotion ahead of my years, a lifestyle ahead of my years, and fulfilment ahead of my years as well.

I'm still an active sportsman making progress; not on the way down, but on the way up at thirty something.

I've got a young family well on the way, and a lifestyle that really I never even dreamed of until I've applied your principles.

You have given me the courage and the tools to grind out the results.

RELATE AND ASSIMILATE

John tires you out just talking to him. He is so 'wired', yet was achieving nothing because of negative thinking, chasing the wrong goals, and by failing to plan he was planning to fail.

He is now so disciplined, because he is focused on his long term goals, and it is the focus which brings the discipline.

*John is now only competing with himself, because, as Baz Luhrman said, '**the race is long, and in the end it's only with yourself**'.*

He is contented, because he has goals, and he really has taken our message on board.

*John is not boastful, though he is evangelical about the potential that lies within all of us, and he really is living proof that, as the great American philosopher Emerson said, '**what lies before us, and what lies behind us, are tiny matters, compared to what lies within us**'*

Write three lessons below that you learned from John:

1

2

3

HAKUNA MATATA

Mike's Introduction

Gayle was one of our first ever course 'guinea pigs', and what an incredible story she has to tell you. The light in this woman's life was about to go out in 1996, yet now it has turned into what George Bernard Shaw called a 'splendid torch'!

We talk, on the programme, about 'putting your own lifejacket on first, before helping others put on theirs'. Gayle shows why this is so important.

You are going to read about a Christmas Day miracle, which you will find hard to believe, yet it's all true, every magical word.

And why, 'Hakuna Matata'? Read on, and find out!

Mike   So, Gayle, you came probably on the very first or maybe only the second course we ever ran, I think it would have been in 1996.

Gayle   I think it was the first one, August.

Mike   So come on tell us about the situation as it was then.

Gayle   The situation as it was then was I'd left work. I'd worked for four years, at ICI, and was the team leader for export distribution, and then my father died. I had two teenage sons and all their issues, which I found really stressful; my husband was away, so I was dealing with all this on my own. As soon as Chris, my husband, came back, I just collapsed!

I had a complete nervous breakdown. It started with panic attacks, which developed, as they quite often do, into agoraphobia, so I wasn't leaving the house, I wasn't answering the telephone or the door, no way!

It got so bad, that I wouldn't even leave one room all day, even if that meant I couldn't have a drink or go to the bathroom. The television was too intrusive, so I just knitted sweaters and did needlepoint, all very introverted things, which was not how I had been. And it got even worse, there were only three people I would talk to in the whole world.

I was on medication, and would stay in bed for days. Eventually I went into hospital. I was in the Psychiatric Unit for 14 weeks.

I underwent a lot of therapy. It was very frightening too. I mean, some of the people in there just do not get better. Initially, it did me more harm than good. It really did terrify me. Initially,

I could not even stay there, yet the doctors said that I was too ill to leave.

Chris would take me in every morning, leave me in a chair, and I would just sit there all day until he came at six to collect me. I would not even move. Eventually I had to stay in, because of the medication; this was a real clinical depression.

There was just no hope; I looked in the mirror and didn't even recognise myself. I then got a room of my own, which was better, because I could shut myself away, but once that happened, at weekends, when I could go home, I didn't want to. I became institutionalised. I was always last to leave, and first back on Monday!

After the 14 weeks I had to go home, but I wasn't much better. I was suicidal; life was just not worth it anymore.

My psychiatrist arranged for me to go to a day centre for 12 weeks, and Chris bought me a Triumph Stag sports car, to encourage me to go. I hardly ever even drove it! I walked all the way instead, even in pouring rain!

Then, one day, almost four years from the start of all this, out of the blue, one of your colleagues rang me.

Mike   *Stop! Did you say four YEARS?*

Gayle   Oh, yes, this went on for a long time. A colleague had been to see me in hospital, and brought her new baby. So anyway, she called, one afternoon; I wasn't even dressed! I told her everything; she said, 'Right! That's it! You're coming on this course!' I said, 'I can't!' But finally I said, 'I'll think about it.' She said, 'No! You must come!'

But I didn't want to be with people, Mike; the problems were insurmountable.

Of course, she was really positive with me, very encouraging, really supportive, and then of course her young son, came on the phone. He said, 'Hakuna Matata!' and I knew he meant 'don't worry' as I had seen The Lion King, and thought, 'Wow', for some reason, that, coming from this child just struck something within me. No adult had done it. So, I agreed to come, and Chris, who was listening, said, 'You'll be fine; I'll take you and collect you.'

Mike   *And did he?*

Gayle   Only the first day; the second day, I drove myself! But Mike, on the first day, I instantly felt comfortable when I came. There was an air of comfort, which I have never experienced on any course since, and that was down to you. As a Counsellor myself now, I have learned the power of empathy and congruence, and that is probably exactly what happened that day. I didn't know that then, and probably neither did you! But you did it!

You touched something in me on a deep level, and all of a sudden, I had something to talk about again, and boy did I talk about it! People became interested in me again!

People started to see the life in me again that they knew was there somewhere, but thought they would never see again. Chris thought he would never have me back again.

In the time between the second and third days, about six weeks, I used the techniques you taught me. Very simple techniques and simple things work. I had some long-term goals to stop smoking and lose weight, to go on holiday. And I did all three! Not in the first six weeks, but I did do all three! And once I had done those, that was it; been on that cruise, lost the weight, and I went on from there.

Mike   *I remember hearing about the cruise, I was amazed!*

Gayle   I went on four last year! I even did one without Chris!

Mike   *We used to talk about you all the time; especially whenever it got tough in here, we used to say, 'Hold on a minute! We have to keep going for Gayle, and the other people, who believe in us, who need us!' So you were brilliant for us too.*

Gayle   I then got involved with the Homeless. I built some great relationships with some really vulnerable people. What you taught me was that this philosophy on life is not a way of **doing**, it's a way of **being**, and it just became easier. Before long, I was making a difference to those people, an old man, whoever. A couple I supported for years, who I met drinking on a market, now they live in a beautiful flat, and they send me the most wonderful cards.

From there I started doing the Soup Kitchen. So then I went to college to find out how I could help these people more. I did my first Counselling course for ten weeks, and really enjoyed that.

W CLEMENT STONE

Then I took the Certificate, which took a year, and I got even more hooked. I then wanted to make a career of it, but the Diploma is £3,000.

Now this is the part that you'll like. Because I had stopped smoking, I had put the money away, every week, and that money paid for the Diploma. It came to £3,600. So this stuff you teach really works, you know!

The Diploma is two years, and I am in no doubt that I will get it. I'm working at Tameside Hospital in Occupational Health, as a Staff Counsellor! My clients are now Nurses, Social Workers, A&E Sisters, Managers, Nursery Nurses, Physiotherapists; a wide range really.

Mike *What a change! What a story!*

Gayle What a journey! Even before all this, I would never have come this far. So my next goal is to work towards my Accreditation, and even though I am not the brightest button in the box I am going to do that too!

Beyond that I plan to study with the girlfriend of Carl Rogers, who teaches Therapeutic Art in California, which is a great way for people with limited vocabularies to express themselves. Then I could work with children too.

But the final part of my story is unbelievable.

Mike *You did fine so far by me!*

Gayle I'm not running the Soup Kitchen myself anymore, but I still cook on Easter Sunday and I do the Christmas Day Breakfast. On Christmas Day, when I arrived, there were two guys stood outside the back door. They didn't look hungry; in fact one was wearing the most beautiful sheepskin coat. I thought I had seen one of them before though.

I went in, and my husband, who had arrived before me said the two guys were asking for me.

I started cooking, and before long one of them came inside, and asked if I was Gayle. He asked if I was organising this 'bash'. It was Bobby Ball, the comedian. He had been asking around to see if anything was being done for the Homeless locally, and

94

had been told about us. He was working in the town at the time. He introduced me to his friend, Keith. I told them they were welcome, but Ball said, 'No, we've come to help.' I was stunned!

They did whatever I asked. I asked him to mix with the guests, so he said, 'Okay, I'll help on the tables, but I want you to go and talk to Keith and tell him what you're doing'. I was busy, but he insisted. I had no idea who the guy was. 'Don't forget,' he said, 'this could be the best thing that has ever happened to you! He thinks you're brilliant. He's watched you with these people, and he thinks you are so good with them.'

However, my priority on Christmas Day is these people, so I carried on working. I expect all the helpers to make it special, not stand in groups talking, and I lead by example.

This guy then approached me and asked how often I did this. I told him about the two days, but told him that following the Counselling training I was completing, one of my goals was to set up a counselling service for the Homeless, because there was nothing for them in Blackpool at all.

'How much would that cost?' he asked. I said, 'I don't know; ten grand?'

'Right' he said, 'it's yours.'

'What is?' I asked.

'Ten grand.' He gave me a scrap of paper. 'That's my office number. Call it on Monday and speak to my secretary. You won't see me again.'

I didn't believe it.

Bobby Ball looked at me. 'You don't realise what's happened to you! God has looked down on you, and a miracle has happened here on Christmas Day.'

I still have no idea who this guy was, but I can set up the service now, and still carry on working.

Mike   *You must be pinching yourself!*

Gayle   You could say that, what with that and everything else; you know this year I flew to America to go on the world's biggest ship, 'Voyager of the Seas', 146,000 tonnes, unbelievable! I had such a fabulous time!

Mike   *Are you back to what you were five years ago, Gayle?*

Gayle	No. Better. I'm better than I was. I'm free, I've had that experience, and I'm not ashamed that I've been there either, I think it was meant; part of the journey, lots of learning, lots of understanding. I don't want to do it again though!
Mike	*People will be so inspired by this!*
Gayle	Mike I think everybody has a growth potential in them; it's not anything we think, or even anything we feel; it's just there. We just need to be nurtured. A potato plant will sprout anywhere, to the best of its potential given its circumstances; I was just fortunate to be given the right circumstances.
Mike	*Did you say 'fortunate'!*
Gayle	Yes, funny eh? I'm more fulfilled; I make a difference Mike. I remember one guy I took in, who had been beaten up by Loan Sharks. He was living rough, mixing with some bad characters. They had taken his Benefit Book so instead of getting £66 each week, he was getting only £16. They fed him alcohol, then dumped him on the street. I asked him, 'Do you want me to help you?' He said there was nothing I could do, that he was finished.

He had 16 pence in his pocket.

He was an old man, but he had been in the Navy for twelve years; had been married with a family, a home, and was a grandfather, yet here he was, in this state. I knew there was something in him. I put him in a holiday flat that night. I went every day, mopped up sick and blood sometimes, and kept him there for three weeks. People gave me money to help keep him there, and then I found him a permanent flat.

I did his washing for him, and one day got a needle stick injury in his flat. I knew he didn't do drugs, so I knew people had been in his flat. In one room, one day, I removed 75 one litre cider bottles. People said I was stupid and that he would never change, but I knew they were wrong. It was just a case of holding him there until he changed.

Anyway, he met a lady, and he's getting married! He listens to her. They have moved into a really nice two bedroom flat, and that is two years on! They aren't all successes, but ones like that make a difference.

I think I was the only friend he had in the world.

I'm not sure you're aware how far the seed that was planted on the first day of your course has spread. It has not only affected my life, but so many others around me too. My son, Andrew, for instance; my other son Justin; all my relationships, with everybody, are just so much better. You know, I was falling out with everyone, avoiding people, and there isn't anyone like that now, and that's just because I decided to change.

Mike, the course is so far reaching, there is a kind of ripple effect, and once you start, it just keeps going. I don't have any great aspirations, I just want to live my life and make a difference for people.

I sleep contentedly every night now. I used to be so full of fear, of people, of driving a car anywhere, of lots of things, and now I'm so brave, so courageous, and so independent.

I know that the experience is enabling me to help others now.

Just finally, by the way, as Bobby Ball and this man, Keith, were leaving the Christmas Day Breakfast something else happened. They stayed until everyone else was going. It was amazing, and as I approached them, I saw this Keith guy taking things out of his pockets, and I said, 'What are you looking for?' I thought he was looking for a pen or some paper to write down his office telephone number for me, 'Nothing,' he said, 'I'm alright.'

Once his pockets were empty, he took his coat off, and said, 'Gayle, give this to one of the lads, it will keep them warm over Christmas.' 'You can't do that,' I said, 'this coat is gorgeous!'

'I've got lots of coats at home; there must be somebody who is going to be really cold today.' And he gave me this coat, and the 'tramp' who wears that coat today stands outside The Winter Gardens in Blackpool, selling The Evening Gazette!

And you know, Mike, I still don't really know who this guy is. I have had to call his office twice, and I can't even catch the name they use when they answer the phone. It's a Preston number, but that's all I know.

Mike   *Gayle, maybe you never will know, who cares! You just proved to us that **miracles do happen, to those who believe!** Thank you.*

RELATE AND ASSIMILATE

How do you follow a story like that? I don't know what challenges you are facing right now, but if they are greater than the ones Gayle faced, I would be amazed.

This woman is an inspiration to anyone who is going through a tough time, so draw strength from her story.

*What did it say to me? **The bad times make you stronger.** I need to remember that, personally. Gayle is grateful for the lessons she learned, and will face future adversity in a different way, with more calmness and confidence in her power to influence the eventual outcome.*

***You never know where your lucky break is going to come from.** I was once told to treat every person I ever met like the one who was going to give me the key to my fortune. Look at the way Gayle relates to the Homeless people she meets; I found that so humbling. Aren't people fantastic? Of course they are; they all are.*

Gayle, I promise you now that I will never walk past a Homeless person again without a kind word and the gift of some change from my pocket.

Thank you for pricking my conscience.

What did Gayle say to you?

1

2

3

Gayle's Story

`You never know where your lucky break is going to come from.´

Gayle, a true inspiration to us all.

'DEAD EASY THIS!'

Mike's Introduction

Dave is an incredible person. He is very laid back in his style, and has absolutely no 'airs and graces', he's just a straight forward kind of guy. When he came on his course, as you will find out, he was a heavy smoker, with a lifetime habit.

Let him tell you what he did, and prepare to be amazed!

Mike   *How long was it in to the course before you actually started thinking 'there's something in this'?*

Dave   I think in the first two hours it was very 'getting to know the people around you' because you do get different mixes of people around you. Some things you don't wish to reveal. After we had coffee in the morning you started talking about a few different principles and then after lunch when you started talking about the subconscious mind and the brain, that's when I started to think 'there's a bit more to this.'

Mike   *Was its impact immediate for you?*

Dave   Well, I left my girlfriend a crazy message at the end of that first day, and, in all honesty when I came back from the course on the second day, Geraldine was crying! I was saying, 'hey look at this', getting my books out and she was thinking 'bloody hell!'

Mike   *What was it that made her cry?*

Dave   I think it was because I was really happy for some reason. I was very much, you know, "I've got a new direction here", because, about April or March time I was thinking of leaving my job for something new. When I'd been on the course it made me realise, 'hang on, what you want is right here, why go somewhere else and do something new when you can do it here. Stop looking round and do this!' I started relating those principles to it - I've gone to Germany and done a cracking job over there!

Mike   *Was her reaction caused by seeing you so happy and the power of your feeling?*

Dave   Yeah, I think she thought I was a like a different person.

Mike   *Did you think that?*

Dave   No, I just thought I'd woken up a bit you know, thought I was realising that I'd a lot to do still, got a lot of potential. It was really good. She was alright in the end. She's thought about it

	a lot and read my self help books which are always lying around now. She's walking around the kitchen and there will be one of my sayings stuck on the back of the door about 'Self Belief' or something!
Mike	*What's your current favourite one?*
Dave	Current favourite one is '**keep your mind on the things that you want and off the things that you don't want and that way you end up with a burning desire**'.
Mike	*Is that Napoleon Hill?*
Dave	Yes, that's Napoleon Hill.
Mike	*When I first met Art Niemann in 1992 he gave me some posters and I've still got them at home and one of the ones I still use now, a yellow one, is '**keep your mind on the things you want**' – it's very powerful, just that simple phrase.*
Dave	Those two words, '**burning desire**', hit me straight away!
Mike	*So what did you apply this to, when you finished the course?*
Dave	First thing I did was to give up smoking – I've been smoking for about 15 years.
Mike	*How many a day?*
Dave	20 a day, and I've been on Benson & Hedges and switched to Silk Cut and things like that. The thing that did it for me was when you said 'do not leave this room and throw your cigarettes away – that isn't going to work', and I thought 'OK this is pretty cool. What a great way to give up smoking! You can carry on smoking while you do it!' So I thought to myself 'fine', and looked at the techniques. I had a time in my mind when I wanted to give up so after the course I came home and I promised my girlfriend I'd give up smoking in four weeks.
Mike	*Does she smoke?*
Dave	No! I thought, every time I light up I'm going to say to myself 'why are you doing this? You don't smoke; why have you got a cigarette in your hand?' I made myself go downstairs to smoke. We lived in a three storey house so every time I wanted a cigarette I had to go downstairs to the utility room to have my cigarette.
Mike	*You made the whole thing feel negative?*
Dave	Oh yeah, having to go downstairs, having to come back all the way back upstairs. If I wanted to have a cigarette I'd have to

stop the video or miss my television programme. After about two weeks, I was really beginning to hate it. Every time I went downstairs I felt guilty because of the 'dendrites' I was building in my brain.

In the third week, I noticeably smoked less and all it needed then was the final push – I thought, 'Thursday that will be it'.

On the Monday before the Thursday I was going to the newsagents to buy more cigarettes, and I didn't even want to go there. I was thinking 'Right, Thursday these will be gone'. I'd booked a restaurant, smoked all day Thursday until 5 pm, went to the restaurant, had a nice meal and Geraldine said 'what is it you're celebrating then?' And I said, 'have you not noticed?' When she realised, she couldn't believe it! Friday went by and I was thinking 'great'. I got in to work and I found myself standing up to go for a cigarette and I thought 'I don't do that' so I sat down again and carried on working! It must have looked really weird!

Mike	Did you feel good about yourself for doing that?
Dave	Really good, it was like I knew it was just something that wasn't me anymore just because I told myself.
Mike	You'd told yourself that many times?
Dave	Well you light up about 20 times a day, so there are 20 times when you can say to yourself – 'what are you doing this for?' Now it is dead easy because every time I see someone who is smoking, people say 'how can you walk in here and see people smoking?' And I can say, 'well I don't do that – what a complete waste of time!' So on the Saturday I was watching TV and my daughters sat in front of the television, I thought what we need now is some coloured cards and pictures for 'triggers'.

I was drawing like a kid again – two red balls connected like a dumbbell – drew it all over the page with the words 'choose oxygen' with pictures of oxygen molecules. The next time I felt like a cigarette, I'd look at it.

I only needed that for about four hours in the evening. That was the turning point for me. There was a section in your notes from the course on one of the very first pages and it says 'what would you dare to do if you knew you couldn't fail?' I thought 'I'd stop smoking', and so I stopped smoking. Some of the 'IDs' I've got now really frighten the life out of me!

Mike	Because they are so powerful?

Dave	That's right yes, I'm looking at some of them and thinking 'can I really try this?' Some of them that I have got right now are pretty fantastic – and another thing on the card said – 'I want to be a singer' – everyone can sing – to a degree.
Mike	*Yes and it's true. I was reminding someone the other day that one of the biggest selling artists at Blackpool Opera House (and they've had Tom Jones, Frankie Vaughan, Shirley Bassey) is Jane McDonald – the lady who worked on a cruise ship. Anybody can do it!*
Dave	You know the 'IDs'? On your course you show us what to do, what to write, and you attach an emotion to it, and I had to ditch a couple of them because I couldn't attach an emotion to them. So you think of another way to do it, and get a different emotion, but I knew when I gave up smoking that someone else had done it for me. I really felt that my subconscious mind had done it. That's how easy it was to do. I've tried to give up three or four times; I'd buy nicotine gum, stuff like that, plastic cigarettes, even the patches – the only thing that the patches cause is the dreams at night because when you're smoking you get the rush of the cigarette! There are new pills that are meant to just switch off the craving in the mind!

TABLETS OF STONE 6
KEEP YOUR MIND ON THE THINGS YOU DO WANT
AND OFF THE THINGS YOU DO NOT WANT

W CLEMENT STONE

Well I knew that what I learned on your course was so powerful and the night before I was really looking forward to it to be able to tell the class.

I came all the way back from Germany purely for it!

At work now, whenever we get a problem, I'll just say, '**No, Dead Easy this!**'

When I'm at home and I haven't got time to do something I say to myself, 'yes I have – dead easy this!' I use it as a self starter all the time now.

TABLETS OF STONE 7
TO MOVE ONE TO ACTION, DESIRE MUST BE JOINED
TO AMBITION AND INITIATIVE

W CLEMENT STONE

When I went to Germany there were things there that would have put some people off going; for a kick off I couldn't speak a word of German!

I'd been there once for a weekend; I could order two pints of beer and that's it! I said to myself 'dead easy this'. Anyway I got over there and there were some tough things and on the first week I was thinking to myself 'have I done the right thing?'

Then the day after I thought I'll do things that I would never have done before. I was working over there for four months away from home as well, left my girlfriend at home. And it was dead easy. I used to go home after these tricky meetings and I used to think to myself – 'dead easy this' – do my homework for the meetings understand their requirements and said 'dead easy', over and over, just trained myself for the meetings!

I remember an ISO auditor came over about the second week I was there and said 'can you show me your records for this' and all these records were in German so I thought 'OK'. We got the ISO approval through based on what we had showed them and I was the only person there that he'd talked to who was English. At the end of it he said, 'I've got to tell you I don't envy you it must be hard this with a foreign language in a foreign country' and I said 'no, it's dead easy'. He said 'was it not overwhelming or anything like that?' and I said 'no not at all; nothing is too hard'.

Mike	*Has it made you more aware of people around you thinking negatively?*
Dave	Oh yes, you see it a mile off, as soon as you've been on the course. One of the first things you say is that you'll recognise negative self talk and it's all around you, it's everywhere.
Mike	*One good thing I notice is that even people in your company who haven't been on the course know that negativity no longer works! Especially if **you** are in the room!*
Dave	You have to be realistic and have to balance, but we don't enjoy thinking negative thoughts. You see people who have reacted well and you see people who have reacted differently and you compare them to all the people who have put their minds to it and taken it on board - they're different people they really are! They are much better to work with, much better.
Mike	*Dave, what would you say to somebody who was going to come on the course outside of the company, or if someone is reading this book now, what would be your message to them?*

Dave	I reckon that for me it has been one of the biggest eye openers that I've ever seen. It's taught me a lot about myself that I didn't realise existed. I found it very much a life changing experience – not just changing me, changing my family as well – it's changed my life and my attitude, about how I do things.
	It's better at home as well because sometimes you just can't get motivation to do something and in the course it explains about how to motivate people, how to motivate yourself, and how everything you ever achieve and everything you ever do is down to motivation.
Mike	*Yeah, if you think you won't, you won't, which is such a pity when there is another way.*
Dave	And it's all so much more enjoyable; this course has really done a lot for me because I now do things differently. You know, I go to the bookshops and go to the 'self-help' section!
Mike	*You really don't want to stand in front of that or you might find that you do need help! Do you just go to the shop or do you look on the web?*
Dave	I like to go to the shops to look around and you can mark down the books, the web is obviously easier, but it's good to have a look round the shops.
Mike	*Things always work out.*
Dave	Well, sometimes things do go well and sometimes things do go bad, and there are two ways you can handle it; you can either pick yourself up again or not. Thomas Edison did 10,000 experiments before he came up with the light bulb. 10,000 failures before he succeeded! When we are coming up with solutions for our customers, we'll sometimes come up with some things that won't work. I went home on Friday afternoon and I struggled all weekend with this one particular problem. I was thinking to myself 'there has got to be a way' and on Saturday nothing. Then 4pm Sunday I thought, 'there has got to be something'. Then at 5pm, bang – I got this brainwave, and I'm thinking 'where has this come from?' I strongly believe that it was my subconscious! If you keep your mind on what you want there has got to be a way – there has got to be something. I think your subconscious sends signals out and says – 'let's monitor what's going on' and then you are alerted to little things that otherwise you might have missed.

TABLETS OF STONE 8
WITHIN US WE HAVE THE POWER TO CREATE
A DRIVING FORCE SO SINCERE THAT
ALL OBSTACLES IN OUR PATH ARE REMOVED

W CLEMENT STONE

Mike   *And did you find the answer for the customer?*

Dave   Yes, I mean it was great, because I got my piece of paper out and I was thinking 'yeah that'll suit him!

I'd had a bad day recently and I thought 'what have we done this week?' and I wrote it all down in a big circle. I thought 'we've done all this but we've forgotten about all these achievements and we never gave them a second thought because we'd just done them and taken them for granted' and this one, tiny, little thing had made it into a bad day! No way! Positive thinking, that's what you need. You keep your mind on what you want. All these things this course tells you really work if you just use them.

Mike   *Well you've obviously had an impact on other people because every time I speak to someone they're always talking about you. Do you think it rubs off on people?*

Dave   Yes, I think it probably does. My girlfriend is a good example. She didn't want to go to Germany - she'd been there for nine months before and hated it. When I got there I said to myself 'dead easy this' and there are times when all it needs is for you to say to yourself 'oh no, it's rubbish this', and before you know it, you're booking your aeroplane tickets to 'Everything is Awful'. You don't want to talk to anyone; but - you say to yourself - 'dead easy this' 'I'll have a cracking time' - and you will do!

A couple of hours later we did an Irish bar in a suburb called Schwarbing watching United on telly. If I'd have been negative I believe I wouldn't have enjoyed it at all, but having used positive thinking the time has flown by and I've enjoyed it. I've got a lot of 'IDs' at the moment; learning five new things every day. I'm getting married in May, then I'm going to move to a massive house, get a BMW 325i and I've got one or two others that frighten me a bit!

Mike   *You'll have to keep letting us know how you get on with these. What about your old mates at British Aerospace, what would they do if they could see you now?*

Dave   I don't think they would think I was a different person - still the same person but with different feelings - different attitude.

RELATE AND ASSIMILATE

Dave is extraordinary. Never could you imagine a more changed man, no wonder Geraldine cried! I met her and she first scolded me, then forgave me, then thanked me.

Dave reminds me that positive thought requires no more effort than negative thought, and that positives and negatives infect those around you.

Next time you are faced with a challenge, try Dave's very own self motivator, 'Dead easy this!' I bet it works for you! Of course it's still working for him. What he talks about as 'Inevitable Dreams' (IDs) are goals, and he has achieved so many since our interview.

So, what three lessons did you learn from Dave's story?

1

2

3

'BON APPETIT'

Mike's Introduction

This is a great one. Paul, MBE no less, is a good friend of ours now, an avid Bolton Wanderers fan, and his story is amazing. Paul, a Celebrity Chef with a Michelin Star to his name, is regularly featured in magazines and on TV. He has many restaurants. He cooks for the likes of Sir Alex Ferguson, Mick Hucknall of Simply Red, David and Victoria, Liverpool FC, even Sir Paul McCartney himself, so he has a few tales to tell, and he shares them AND his secret of success. Bon Appetit!

Mike *We first met in Manchester long ago, so it's great now to have had some of your team through our course.*

Paul We shall probably have more if I'm being truthful Mike, we've got a very exciting time coming up and we have to do a lot of training. The whole of the culture of our company is something that I want to drive forward. We've not been very good at doing that, at spreading that success message. Because we were a small company everybody shared success but as we've started to grow bigger that's become diluted, and now I've got to find a way of back tracking a bit, sharing that success, and getting those messages over, telling everybody about how good we are. All that was part of the thought process I got out of you first of all, because from then on I read a lot, and I have seen and heard other speakers. Many things you said were not new to me, they were put in a different and better way, but actually seeing the staff benefit, was really quite exciting.

Mike *What's that been like for you?*

Paul We are a people business; a strong restaurant business depends on that. We have a higher ratio of personnel than probably a lot of other businesses. It accounts for a minimum of 30% of all costs, so that's quite high when you consider that food costs are another 30-35%. So we are a people business and I do believe our social skills are declining. One of the things we found increasingly difficult was getting people who can say hello, give a smile and say goodbye, which makes a massive difference to the customer because some people want to be able to talk to your staff.

Mike *They want to go somewhere where people make them happy, make them feel good or recognise them or say, 'nice to see you again' or whatever it might be.*

Paul Yes, or shaking their hands, Steve Rushton was one who I recognised fairly early would benefit from the course. After doing the three days he was 'awesome', instead of 'alright' whenever he was asked how he was! He was good and he has been up ever since and seeing that was quite a transformation. It made him a much stronger person and better at delegating. As Steve's attitude is more positive it has made a big difference to everyone.

Mike   *Paul, your young staff don't just come to work for the money, so to have a manager who lifts them and lets them feel great when they are there, must make the job a lot easier?*

Paul   Yes, and our industry can be really tough at times. You can get to eleven o'clock at night and you haven't even had time to go to the toilet, so you do need someone lifting you, just to finish that last dinner course. We do need managers who can really lift people at the end of a long day and night. Being a very positive person might seem only a minor thing but for me it's enormous really, because we can teach the other skills, but the social skills, spreading that throughout the business, has been really good.

Mike   *Being in a restaurant around people who want to serve you and who are going out of their way to make sure you have a good time seems really important. Surely you can't afford a customer to see you having your bad moment or off day, whoever you might be, because every moment is critical?*

Paul   We don't have long from a customer placing the order and servicing that order, unlike many other businesses where that might be weeks. So if you get a bad impression straight away when you're in that restaurant we've had it!

Mike   *And most customers probably won't tell you that they won't come back!*

Paul   Probably 90% of people won't; in fact we welcome complaints because at least we've got a chance to turn that round. People don't come back to the restaurant if they have not enjoyed it.

Mike   *But what about you personally, obviously you've been on the course; have you used any of the techniques in your life?*

Paul   I certainly don't say 'alright' anymore! I think probably the most powerful things I found for me were the lifetime goals. Because I've been reasonably successful in a short period of time, time does pass quickly, and you made me realise that time is marching on! I think bringing those goals and timescales into focus, understanding where the children are going to be, realising that they are going to be 15 when I'm going to be 50, put things into perspective. I always have been quite good at moving my goals and achieving them but I've always been looking 3-5 years ahead, but you made me look 25 years ahead!

Mike   *One of the things we talked about when we were doing that exercise was that it is important to keep your life in balance. I always looked to you and thought you were pretty good at that - it's interesting for me to see that it's had an impact on even someone like you who I would say had that pretty much sorted.*

Paul   I think it drives it home in the course though, Mike. I've been used to being fairly organised but I think going on the course helps you set a few more goals, you know, and certainly in the financial aspects.

Mike   *We talk about comfort zones - that position when you are just on the edge of the comfort zone, what a great place that is to be, as opposed to being miles outside it thinking, 'I can't cope'.*

Paul   Well I'm challenge orientated, extremely; in fact I'm not motivated without it; in fact I'm probably hard to live with if I haven't got a challenge in my life.

Mike   *Who do you look up to and what do you admire about them?*

Paul   I think if you were talking about football, I probably admire people like Brian Robson, who perhaps wasn't the most talented of football players. Kevin Keegan might be another one who springs to mind. They worked extremely hard and used every single ounce of everything given to them. They weren't given particularly great attributes, but what they did have, they used more than 100%.

Mike   *Do you think that's also describing you in a way?*

Paul   I would see some of those attributes in me, though I don't have the patience that I admire in, say Nick Faldo! I don't think I've got that patience. I wish I was a Gascoigne and had the same attributes.

Mike   *When you play your squash, is yours a 'grafting' approach or have you got talent?*

Paul   I was coached and I don't think I'm a bad squash player, technically, but yes, when the going gets tough there isn't a thought of losing a game. When it's six all in the fifth set, that doesn't enter my head; I'm thinking the opposition is always more tired than me; that may not always be the case, but I'm always telling myself that.

'Murder on the squash court' by Jonah Barrington was always a good book in my eyes and I still remember it.

Probably the greatest time on a squash court that I've seen, was when Jonah was doing a demonstration, he was supposed to be doing it with a guy called Hiddy Jehana. I think he was about number three in the world at the time. It was on at my father's squash court, and I knew Hiddy hadn't turned up because my father had told me that Jonah had brought someone else – it was a big disappointment.

Jonah walked on to the court, he looked up at the balcony and said, 'Ladies and Gentlemen, I'm very sorry, I know some of you will be disappointed. I was supposed to be doing a demonstration with Hiddy, but his agent wouldn't let him come today, because he's not getting paid and I'm doing this as a favour for Ken Heathcote, and I hope we won't disappoint you. I've brought a young lad along who I am coaching at the moment, he's about number 31 in the world rankings and I'm number seven, I played him in the Irish Open last year and beat him 3-0, but I've been coaching him ever since.'

'I'd just like to tell you that since the Irish Open I've never taken a game off him! That's not a match, in case some of you didn't hear, but a game. I'm talking about not one single game in one single match! This guy is ranked number 31 in the world, but as you will see he's really number two in the world at the moment, but no one else knows that except me *and him*!'

He said, 'he'll play Geoff Hunt in the final of the British Open this year, he will make the final and Geoff will beat him, because he's still just too good for him; but next year he will win the British Open and the World Championship and he will become the greatest player the world of squash has ever seen. I'll be lucky to take a point off him today, I'd like you to welcome 15 year old Jahangir Khan!' The hair stood up on the back of my neck, Mike!

Nobody had heard of this kid, but **everything Jonah said on that squash court came true!**

Jahangir didn't lose a match for seven years! He didn't lose a game in a match for five years! The only game he lost that next year was to Geoff Hunt in the British Open Final, and the following year, he was World Champion, beating Geoff Hunt 3-0, and he never lost a game in 5 years after that! Geoff Hunt went after that and retired from the game, he had internal bleeding! He just drove him out of the game, he ran him out of the game. Nobody in any sport had been that dominant. No-one's held a record like that ever since.

Mike   *And you saw him that day?*

Paul   Yes it was a Sunday afternoon, I remember. I was never so inspired; you could not get me off the squash court after that!

Mike   *Did you tell me once about Barrington's control of a squash ball?*

Paul   I told you I saw him do an exhibition game, where he got the two best players from the club – County standard – and asked them to do some simple exercises which they couldn't do.

He then did one of his very own.

He started at the front of the court and literally held the racquet right up near the head, and he just knocked the ball above the line on the front wall, and then he just slipped his hand down the racquet, and just started to step back and knock it, keeping it on the volley.

He walked all the way to the back of the court and then moved it all the way back to the front.

Then he knocked it back out again, all the way to the very back, opened the glass door at the back of the court, knocked the ball against the front wall one last time, stepped out and caught the ball on his racquet over the top of the glass outside!

TABLETS OF STONE 9
TO BECOME AN EXPERT,
WORK, AND WORK HARD

W CLEMENT STONE

Mike   *So the ball never touched the floor once?*

Paul   Never touched the floor, and what he was demonstrating was that you should have the ability, if you want to be World Champion, to know exactly where that ball is going every single time. It was just one of those magical moments, you know, and it just demonstrates how good you really have to be to be a World Champion – at anything.

Mike	*And he would say, I think I'm right in saying, that he wasn't naturally all that talented?*
Paul	Well he wasn't that talented! His first lesson I think was when he went to see the World Champion, the master who became his mentor. He went over to India and this guy had learned to play in the dark, literally. As a servant in the Empire days he wasn't allowed to play on the squash courts, so he learned to play in the dark because no one would ever imagine that you would play in the dark because the lights were off!
	Jonah turned up to have his first lesson with this guy, and he got hold of Jonah's racquet, took it off him, put it down right in the far corner of the squash court, went to the service box, hit the ball, landed it on the racquet head, and picked up Jonah's racquet, gave it back to him and said, 'when you can do that 100 times consecutively, then come back for your next lesson.'
Mike	*So that was where Jonah got his inspiration and determination from?*
Paul	Apparently he did exactly the same in the second lesson with the backhand serve, then he said, 'come back when you can do that 100 times and then we'll go for your third lesson'. Jonah stood in the middle of the court thinking 'what the hell have I come all the way here to India for to learn from this guy, who's mad!'
Mike	*Listening to you talk, determination and desire seem to be important qualities to you; how would you phrase it?*
Paul	I think there is always something at the back of your mind saying that you don't want to have failure, and whilst you can accept that you're not going to get everything right, the decisions are right at the time. If you do get it wrong, as you do, it makes you learn by that and you move on and you don't make the same mistake again. I think the determination factor is the will *not* to have failure, almost.
Mike	*Do you think that lies within everybody? Do you think everybody could do that if they could just get the picture right?*
Paul	I think yes. I don't particularly consider myself to be a talented chef. I've certainly worked with people who are considerably younger and more talented than I am, but I think what I have is the ability to keep driving myself forward, and look at why they were better than me, and work as hard as they did, and then hopefully move on from that.

I remember turning 'chateaux potatoes', which is a fancy roast potato, with seven or eight sides on it. You turn the potato and it's nice and curvy like a barrel. I remember one of the lessons going to Sharrow Bay, thinking I was a pretty competent chef.

We literally did two full sacks of potatoes every morning, and in theory it's probably a two hour job, but there was one lad there who could do it in an hour and I used to try and keep up with him. I'd get bloody cuts all over me and I remember watching and thinking 'I've got to be able to turn these equally as good and equally as fast' and it took me six months but in the end I did it. I wasn't going to give up.

He was probably a more naturally gifted chef than I was, but he hasn't been as successful as I have.

Mike   *Sometimes that much talent is perhaps a curse in a way.*

Paul   Perhaps it can be, you can rely on it too much sometimes. Maybe, you know, Robson certainly had talent, but he was no Glenn Hoddle, yet who was more successful?

Mike   *It's not always just about the talent is it?*

Paul   Well it's about your overall makeup; and the most talented footballers don't always make it.

I worked for Raymond Blanc at Sharrow Bay and at the Connaught, and the Connaught was a very, very disciplined kitchen; 15 people in that brigade, and it was hard. It was the SAS of kitchen brigades; it was dog eat dog; it was really only a place for lions, it wasn't a place for mice. As a trainer you wouldn't recommend that, but it's a bit like being in the army, you do as we say, sink or swim, and if you're going to sink we're going to make sure you're going to sink properly. It's a bit of a hard thing to get your head around as a young lad, but you either learn to develop or you don't.

I actually remember sitting on a train at 11 o'clock at night coming back to South London where I was living. I'd just managed to catch the last train, taken earache all night off a second chef who hated my guts, and I'd worked my butt off from before six in the morning. I'd done that on many days I have to say, but I'd just taken so much from him in the kitchen that day, that I just broke down and cried all the way home on the train!

Mike   *How old were you then?*

Paul   23, and I got the train to Brixton, and Brixton isn't the most salubrious of places, stood there at an all night bus stop until one in the morning, got the bus which took me to Norbrook, which was only a couple of miles up the road, and I got in about 1.30 am. I had to be up at 4.30am to go back in to work!

I got up at 4.30 that morning and thought 'I'm not going to take this any longer. The next person that gives me any, will find out what it's like', and I remember strapping somebody down that night on to the hot plate.

I think he was going white or red in the face, I'm not sure which, and it took about three people to pull me off!

I'm not surprised that no one gave me any hassle from then on, and I remember that was very much a turning point in my career.

Whilst I still got some abuse here and there, nobody was going to push that much further any longer, and suddenly things improved.

I used to get better jobs and I had respect in the kitchen and suddenly life became a little easier. I didn't work any fewer hours, but it was a damned site easier, you know, in some respects.

I'd come from that kind of environment, cooking three boxes of spinach for five minutes in a big kind of boiler, freshening the spinach to cool it down, to keep its green colour, and draining it all out.

I went to Raymond Blanc's, where it was suddenly five litres of spinach for three or four **seconds** and I couldn't quite understand that because I'd been used to getting the preparation ready, having it all ready, and Blanc said everything had to be done, and it has to be as fresh as it possibly can be, and it's got to go out on the plate there and then.

He got his hands in front of me, and he put his hands by the side of my eyes, and said, 'you don't act like a racehorse, and don't be blinkered', you know. He took his hands away and said, 'look there is a lot more outside there'.

He said several things, one about - 'there is a fine line between being not just good and excellent, but being absolutely brilliant; there is such a fine line.' He held out his hand and he put it right in front of my eyes so I could see virtually nothing, and he said, 'it's blurred, isn't it?' He said, 'it's such a fine line'. And the other thing he used to do - a simple one - was he used to make you taste all the time, taste and taste and taste and taste. Once I was on the fish section and I had a couple of fish scales which were on the skin of the fish, and I cooked this fish with the fish scales on, and they're not particularly pleasant things.

He found out, then he went and got a raw fish and scraped off all the fish scales, got a big teaspoon and stuck them in my mouth and said 'what do you think of the taste? Do you want to eat them?' Course I didn't bloody want to eat them because they're horrible! And he just said, 'well don't make my customers eat them, because not only that, you're getting yours for free - they've got to pay £18 for this!' So they're lessons that you learn that stick in your mind forever.

Mike   *But if you as a person weren't positive, you couldn't cope with that could you?*

Paul   It would put you under wouldn't it! I just took it as a positive lesson, you know, and he was perfectly right to do that in my mind, because I was serving fish scales, maybe only one or two, but one or two was very important to that dish. It was almost a perfection type thing, but it was just his way of saying, 'let's get it right'.

They were great learning curves for me, massive learning curves really, because nobody had done it that way before.

Mike   *Do you reflect that forward into what you look for now when you are looking for a member of staff in a kitchen - a great attitude to learning and excellence? How important does that weigh in your recruitment?*

Paul   I think we look for common sense, and for people who want to learn, rather than the one who is best qualified. One of the things we have never done is employed pastry chefs and pastry chefs generally speaking in the kitchen tend to be prima donnas. They are the people who think the kitchen owes them a living! No offence to pastry chefs!

Technically pastry is more difficult. Cooking the sauces or meat is a bit more from the heart, pastry is more technically or theory minded, but I've never seen it in that light. If a bloody pastry chef can do it, then I can do it!

Mike   *It comes back to attitude again. Paul, you have two young children; in terms of what you know about being positive, what would you want for them, if you could give them something; a gift of something, what would you give them?*

Paul   I think it would be that all round social skill your course teaches, I mean I think we are very fortunate. Both my wife Gabby and I are in a position to pay for their education. But actually what I feel is that even if they don't come out with any qualifications, as long as they are well rounded people that communicate with otherpeople, interact at all levels of social status, then that's the greatest gift I would want for them.

Paul's Story

AiM HiGH & work Hard

Being the best takes hard work,
and he should know.

Desire. Determination to succeed no matter what it takes, no matter what the obstacles, that's Paul. He's telling us to aim high and not hide behind a lack of natural talent. He's telling us the value of being able to work with others, those social skills of communicating and inspiring. He's saying that being the best takes hard work, and he should know.

Follow his example.

List three lessons Paul gave you:

1

2

3

LIFEJACKET

Mike's Introduction

Amusingly, to me at least, and somewhat irreverently, I thought it was great that I was in a police station, and I was the one doing the interviewing! (Who said 'for a change'?) Pretty cool that. Yet, this guy, what a star he is. He was drifting apparently when he came through the course, and four years later, he looks like he's going all the way.

So, why 'lifejacket'? Well, read the story and you tell me.

Me   *So you went on the course - what happened?*

Mike   I went on the course and I kept saying to the person who had invited me, 'don't send me, send all these other miserable types', but he said 'no, I think you'll really get a lot out of it' and I did.

    I realised that there were so many limiting things that I was doing outwardly. Now I know what my aim is - to be Divisional Commander. My visualisation reverts to when I was a small boy visiting my first office. I remember thinking 'oh my, what a job, what an office, what a fantastic place to be!', and every time I smell real coffee, I'm in there and coffee is laid out for a guest, **my** guest, because it's **my** room.

    The great thing about that is how often do you smell real coffee? All the time! And that means I'm picturing my goal, my dream if you like over and over!

    I've always been ambitious, but I didn't realise I was limiting myself. I was an Inspector for ten years, which is quite a long time, you know. Generally speaking that should be two or three years if you're ambitious.

    Something I used to do, I don't know whether other people do it, but if I've been walking along the street, and there would be a lamp post coming up, and then there is a car behind me, I'd say, 'if I reach that lamp post before the car, I'll get promotion and if I don't I won't'. I'd be running and I'd be saying, 'I'm going to reach that lamp post; if I don't I'll never get promotion!' and sometimes the car would beat me and I'd say, 'see, it's not going to happen!' How crazy is that?

Me   *And that's from a person who thinks he's a positive person!*

Mike   I walked in there on your course and said 'I'm positive', but I was doing all these stupid things to myself all the time, limiting myself! I've never done it since, NEVER ONCE.

I know now if I look after myself, I also can look after other people properly. I can do it much better as a Superintendent, who has the ear of a lot of people and is well respected in the Constabulary. With the help of likeminded people Mike, I'm transforming this Constabulary you know, I'm changing it on a daily basis; WE are changing it! There are so many things now, as I look round this Constabulary, not just in my own Division either, which are so much better.

Me   *You're not talking about the Division, but the Constabulary?*

Mike   I'm going to show you something when we go back in, and it's called 'Sleuth' and I am making all that happen. I'm going to show you how many hits there are; there are not far short of a million hits on 'Sleuth', just within the Constabulary – 715,000 hits on our own intranet, from nothing! What impact, and that's what you can do if you look after yourself and you believe; but if you don't believe, you really will annoy people, and don't go around saying how good you are either, that's even more annoying! For example, I'm talking to you about what's in my head and I know I am achieving because of the way I'm doing things, but I don't boast about that, I just get on with it. I'm telling you for your book, to show people they have to do the same.

Me   *Presumably, what you're saying is that in previous years, you would have put a limit on it and said, 'oh, I'd better not do that, it's a bit risky'.*

Mike   I wouldn't have even set out! Well, number one I wouldn't be in the influential position I'm in now; I wouldn't have been seen as somebody who got things done. The one thing I've done since the course is promote myself more. I started to work out that I'd always spent a lot of time looking after the people who I look after instead of myself. In fact it was something of a badge of honour if the bosses thought I was an idiot!

Me   *I suspect that a lot of that goes on in the world.*

Mike   Yes, what I did was I started to realise that I was just limiting myself. You think it's a badge of honour, and the people who I'm working for let you think that's great, but they don't really!

What they want is someone who they know has got the ear of the organisation and someone who is also good. Well if they get someone who has got the ear of the organisation who is a complete idiot and self centred then people don't want to work for him or her; but people DO want to work for someone who looks after them, who cares for them, and is really powerful in the organisation; who can make things happen for them.

All that became very clear to me, that I've got to manage down and manage up; and it's the managing up that I became much better at.

I remember when I was in the Scouts as a kid with my pal Michael Gerard, that one day the Skip came to see us because he was forming a new patrol. Anyway, the Skip said, 'I want a new patrol leader for Owl patrol', so instead of saying, 'I'm your man', what do I say? 'Michael Gerard's good Skip'. Can you believe that?

Skip comes to offer me the job, and I throw it away! I told the Skip Gerard was better than me, when the Skip wanted me, otherwise he would have asked Gerard himself!

Then it dawned on me that I really wanted the job. I realised that you can look after others, and still look after yourself too.

I should have said, 'Thanks Skip, I know Michael's a good lad too, and that you could have asked him, but I'm really proud that you asked me, and I'm going to do a cracking job for you.'

Sadly that wasn't the last time I got it wrong. People get it wrong all the time. I had one today on an Assessment Centre.

One of my guys let one of the others get away with a silly statement in a group discussion, and I was observing. I asked him why he did it and he said that he didn't want to make the other guy look foolish. Now management and leadership is all about being able to confront people and situations and be courageous, AND do all that in a sensitive, positive way without creating fear or resentment.

TABLETS OF STONE 10
DO THE RIGHT THING BECAUSE IT IS THE RIGHT THING TO DO, REGARDLESS OF THE PERSONAL CONSEQUENCES

W CLEMENT STONE

Me   *Do you remember telling us on the course about your letters? That was a great example of limiting behaviour, and one of the funniest!*

Mike   Well, I always thought I was bad at finishing things off, so I'm no good at doing letters. So whenever I got up to 'yours sincerely' – I couldn't finish it! I had drawers full of 95% written letters!

Me *Well how many letters have you sent since the course?*

Mike Loads! E-mail too – it's email now. There is a group of people that I went to university with, and I am still the only one of my peer group who writes regularly to the rest. One pal, Chris Foreman said, 'I wish I could be a good letter writer like you', and that was before my course, so they still thought I was a good letter writer, but I was telling myself I was hopeless!

Me *It is common for a person to have a lower opinion of themselves than other people have of them! How do people react to you and your style as a person? Do you think they see you as being a catalyst for change?*

Mike Yes, I know now that I've got a great reputation in the Constabulary whereas people (at one time) may have said differently. I'm nationally recognised now. I got a phone call yesterday from a guy in Dumfries and Galloway. He said, 'I've been in touch with a lot of people and they say that you're the person I've got to come to'. He rang my office, he didn't ring the Chief Constable, didn't ring his own headquarters. He rang me in a division in another force; the message was clear: 'you're the man'.

Put self belief and this stuff together and it will drive change. One of my colleagues, Duncan, raised something the other day about reinforcement of your material.

Me *It is crucial.*

Mike We have lost that a little, because I didn't have a clear picture about reinforcement. I thought that if I could have a critical mass - I mean we've got the critical mass in the management team, because everybody on our management team goes on your course, because they can't come on to our management team and not do it. I thought the critical mass was enough - but you need to work on your attitude and your goals all the time.

Me *So if someone is reading this and thinking of coming on the course, what would you say?*

Mike I'd say **JUST DO IT**. When our new Chief Constable arrived, I explained how good it is. I know it works, it changes your life. So I'd say, 'do you want to change your life? If you do, then go on this course. If you don't, then don't bother.' It is energising, life-changing, it just changes every single waking moment from the minute you learn it, until the end, doesn't it?

Me   *Whatever you say, Mike!*

RELATE AND ASSIMILATE

What a top, top man. If you run a business, listen to his wisdom on leadership. In industry that man would earn a fortune, and he only really admitted to himself how good he was, and learned to use his talent to everyone's benefit, following the course.

*That is scary, because if people like **him** undervalue themselves, what hope for the rest of us! Don't let his tone appear boastful either, bullish yes definitely, but Mike is fighting back from hiding his light under a huge bushel for years, and he is sending a message to people through this story, telling them, whoever they are, never to make that mistake.*

*It's a mistake I made when I was sixteen, and modesty cost me a dream. I was 32 when I learned the same lesson, and I have never looked back since. Marianne Williamson wrote, '**when you let your own light shine, you unconsciously give others permission to do the same**'. You have to put your own lifejacket on before you can help another person. It's a simple message, but a powerful one.*

Make sure you follow Marianne's, and Mike's example, by shining.

What were the lessons from this story?

1

2

3

'WHO WANTS TO BE A MILLIONAIRE?'

Mike's Introduction

I took my life in my hands meeting this character on April Fools' Day, anything could have happened!

So who wants to be rich out there? You? Well this guy did, but he had got himself into a big mess, so we told him to hang on to his dream. How did it work out for him? Did he make it? Is it possible?

Read on!

Mike	*Tell us how you came to be on the course in the first place.*
Allan	I did it through a company I was running. Having known you for so many years, I think I had always been interested in what it was that you were all about, and I thought it would be really good to try and change some of the attitudes of some of the guys that worked for the company, and that also I could benefit from it myself at the same time. So if you recall, I contacted you and we set that course for about eight people.
Mike	*What do you recollect about sitting there and listening to it all?*
Allan	I think it was just how positive you were! It screamed out that just having a positive outlook on life can change you, and the way you think about yourself and the things that are important to you, to your business, family, whatever; and that really benefited me. I feel that even now, today, this self esteem thing; I think I had quite low self esteem at the time and it helped me to improve that.
Mike	*Do you mean the awareness of self-esteem?*
Allan	No, the insight into it. You taught me to just do things for yourself, rather than to try and please everybody else all the time. I mean small things like that did make me feel better in myself, and I stopped having a downer on myself all the time.
Mike	*See, that's interesting, because people would look at you, and wouldn't know you that well, yet say 'well look at him, he is the director of a company, lives in a posh house, got a lovely wife, flash car to drive around in', and you would be the last person they'd expect to say 'my self esteem is low'.*
Allan	It's knowing what you want, and as you say I was very lucky, I should be grateful, I have nice a house, lovely wife, lovely kids, but there was still something missing.

Mike	*The thing about you, is that you have the nice house, and you have a good job, because you are a talented guy, aren't you, you earned all that! It's not like I would think that you look at yourself and think that you were lucky to get this or that, or worry that one day someone would find you out.*
Allan	A lot of it is through hard work though Mike and I have always, I believe, felt that I had had a positive attitude, certainly since I came back from working abroad. Since then through all the opportunities that presented themselves, I thought 'yes I can go for this', but even so, deep down inside, there was that fear.

Anyway, the course did the trick. I just changed the aspect of not being so hard on myself all the time, I used to put pressure on myself to be as good as the next person or better than the next person, and in the end I thought I did not have anything to prove, and it was difficult, because I had persuaded the other directors to send the senior management on the course.

The managing director was invited along to the first two hours, and then he bailed out, so I was not getting their buy-in to it. But having said that I could see the reaction of some of the people on the course as being very positive, and I was also listening to some of the sceptics on the course and I ended up trying to sell the course to them. I knew because of your background how fervently you believed in it, and that there must be something in it, and sure enough there was. I really, really enjoyed it. I wouldn't analyse it too deeply but you know I got a warm feeling, the 'feel good' factor, but I am not that into the psychology bit to try and dissect it; it doesn't matter to me as long as it works.

When you said 'you can be whatever you want in life, you can have whatever you want, you can do whatever you want', I knew what I wanted; **I wanted to be a millionaire**; but I laughed it off as if it was a pipe dream. I don't know if just thinking or saying that to yourself makes it happen, but maybe something in the mentality of the way you sow things gives much greater potential for that to happen.

Mike	*So tell us about what has happened in your life since? You had a major crisis in the company, didn't you?*
Allan	There was a lot of politics. To understand the story you need to understand how much I have put into buying into the business of which I was then Director.

I put up the bulk of the equity that we had in the house, I took that out and put it into the business, bought 10% of the business, and then it all started going wrong and I was seriously worried, panicked.

Mike   *You had a big mortgage then?*

Allan   Yes, a £200,000 mortgage on a house that cost £250,000. I had put £140,000 into the business; so you can see from that, that if I had not put that money in, I could have gone and done a £40,000 job.

So it all went wrong in a big way. There were three directors in the business and then me; two of them decided they could not get on with the other guy who was then managing director, (MD), and they asked me if I would help them and become MD if they could oust the current MD.

I agreed on the understanding that both the other two directors resigned and became consultants on a three day a week basis. Basically the business could not afford to have them there full time on the salaries that they insisted on taking out of the business. They were not value for money and the business could not afford to carry them.

So anyway I agreed to do the MD's job. After four months I confronted them and said I thought they were supposed to be bailing out and taking a back seat. I never really got a straight answer, but it was evident that they had no intention of taking a back seat and would continue to take as much money for as long as they possibly could.

That was discouraging at the time; we had had good times for three or four years, but we were on a down slope. I had the financial director whispering into my ear every five minutes, that this was all a disaster and doom and despondency all the time.

He had a vested interest.

When you analyse it now, everybody had a vested interest in it and it was all political!

I was very frightened that all I had worked for, and the lifestyle that I had obtained, even though I was working 70-80 hours a week, was . . . well, in a way I was thinking, I would have to take my daughter out of private school, I would have to sell the house that we had worked hard for, and then move back North and take backward steps and start again! Whilst my wife was someone who was very positive about it, I could not handle it. I could not handle the thought of going back with my tail between my legs. Anybody else probably would not have noticed, but I knew about it, so I could not face that possibility right now.

So I decided I had to do something about it. I started working overtime, thinking about how I could extricate myself from the mess. I got a lot of support from a guy, John that I had never dreamt would help as much. I still do not really know why he supported me as strongly as he did, but I am eternally grateful to him for that support.

It was one of those things that you cannot plan. You would never have dreamt that two people fundamentally so different could get together and take a business to where we took it.

What happened was that in the summer when all these difficulties had manifested themselves, John and I decided we would try and take one of the company's existing contracts, an Irish contract which I had been involved in developing. Given that the other directors were not really interested at all in what was going on in Ireland, there was a fair possibility that if I went to them with a proposal to say, resign, take myself off the payroll, and take two or three highly paid people with me, that I could swing a deal with them to take this contract and start up a new company.

When we took up this contract, we had about 17 people, involved on the job, who we hired in for a company called Lucent. The contract itself was probably worth about £2 million a year. It was going to take three quite well paid guys to help John and me run this business, and then we were going to try and grow it from there. So, first, in October, we started trading in Ireland, put our heart and soul into it and it took off.

I cannot explain to people how difficult it was, for two guys who were basically off the street with no money. I had a £30,000 redundancy payment from the Communications business, but I put the money straight in to the new business!

Between us we probably put £50,000 into the business. We ran the business like an investment and whacked a variety of our personal credit cards for months! It's a good story, that John had a £10,000 limit on his credit card and his wife went out to do the Christmas shopping and the card got rejected! She rang him up and said 'why has the card been rejected?'

He had been paying the wages with the credit card; that was why!

We probably had about £50,000 of credit on cards! One of the things you do not do in business, you do not run your overdraft on an interest rate of 29%! We just did not have any alternative, so we did it, and we became outstandingly successful. Even now I think about it and I think I really do not know how that happened but it did! I heard one of the Dragon's did the same thing!

We started on 1st October, and we were advised at the end of 12 months, to extend our year end to the end of December, but basically we finalised our first year accounts in a 15 month accounting period.

So the first year/fifteen months, turnover went to £23 million!

Mike   *£2 million to £23 million in fifteen months! It shows what can be done though doesn't it?*

Allan   Yes it does, and again I think there was no real ego to contend with, just John and me thinking, 'do it!' - and he has got his wife and two young daughters, and I have two young kids as well. It was like you were doing it for each other and for them. I suppose in some ways that made it even more successful, because we had nobody trying to make a quick buck out of it.

Mike   *So, your dream of being a millionaire came true after all?*

Allan   Well yes, it did.

Mike   *Look back to the point where you were wondering if you would have to sell the house, a couple of years ago . . .*

Allan   Yes, big changes since then.

        I think we have been extremely lucky. I certainly believe that there has been a huge amount of luck involved in it, but then again you make your own luck, you're going to say, aren't you?

Mike   *Don't you just!*

Allan   Well, yes you do. I suppose I'm trying to not take any credit again, aren't I?

Mike   *What does Gary Player say? 'the harder I work, the luckier I get.' Come on Allan, take some credit!*

Allan   Some people do work hard and some people do not. Some wait for the right break, and they are dependent on the luck and if they do not get the luck, they are finished. But some people say, 'if I do that then I might get a break', that's what you mean, yeah?

I am sure some people approach it that way. In my story, if you like to call it a story, the decisions were made for me to an extent, because like I said, I was frightened and I had to do something, and it was born out of desperation.

Mike   *But many people's achievements are. When you look at and analyse a lot of people's achievements, most of them are born out of desperation. Until they actually have one foot over the precipice, people won't start to be daring, brave and courageous, they will be cautious.*

When you are over the precipice, that comfort is gone. Now all of a sudden, the creativity, the energy, the passion, the determination, all comes out! You have no alternative, now you are playing for your life! That is when you find out how good you are!

Allan   It has been like a roller coaster ride these last 18 months. It has been really exciting, because I felt that these are my ideas and, let us see how far they can run. They may not run very far, or you never know, we may be sitting here in a couple of years time say with £300 million!

Mike   *People will be reading this book, maybe even listening to this interview at sometime in the future. Some will skim it, because they do not want what you wanted, others will say, 'this is me'. This is your opportunity to send that person reading the book a message.*

Allan   Basically, what I would say to them is, there are always better things around the corner and you have to get around the corner. Once you are there it is a bright new day. Or can be. It is not necessarily about business, it can be anything in your life. Get over the obstacle, and once you are over it, you wonder what the obstacle was.

**'What lies before us
And what lies behind us
Are tiny matters
Compared to what lies within us'**

Ralph Waldo Emerson
Harvard, Philosopher

Mike   *So, I am sitting there now, and I have just been made redundant, and I am reading this story; what are you going to say to me?*

131

Allan	Believe in yourself, do what you want to do, do what you need to do. There is a lot of luck involved, but make it happen, don't wait and hope; do it!
Mike	*Do you still look at your original Life Goals that we wrote?*
Allan	I have got all the stuff that we did on the course, and to be totally honest with you, I knew I could do it.
Mike	*On the course, I gave you that big book and told you that I was going to show you how to design the future. You looked at me a little weird, but when you did that exercise, you were like a little kid, with all the coloured pens, and people were looking at you, thinking 'what is wrong with him?' There were sparks flying off the end of your pens! And you were saying, 'I am just designing my future mate'. Do you remember that?*
Allan	Yes, I do, and I had never done anything like that before, I don't think most people have. It took me a while, but I got the mortgage paid off! That was one of my big goals, or 'Inevitable Dreams' as you taught me to call them. Things come true. If I can remember correctly, I put on a date to achieve that, which at that time would have been a fantastic achievement, and beat the deadline by 7 years!
Mike	*The reason for that is that when you are actually feeling pretty low, you lose sight, you do an inaccurate audit of your potential and lose sight of your true ability, which causes you to be pessimistic!*

Whatever you can dare or dream; begin it
Boldness has mystery, magic and genius in it

Goethe

Allan	Yes and I think it was good that we had adversity, because it brings more power out of you. I understand that now.
Mike	*You would think that adversity would bring you down, but instead it boosts you up, if you stay positive through it, and so you do come through the other end.*
Allan	It does frighten you, actually; you wonder how far you can go.
Mike	*Where are the limits? Where are the limits for everyone? In their comfort, I hope everybody who reads this, will sit there and think, 'where are my limits' and if you can ask yourself that, you will realise that you can certainly do a lot more than you think you can do.*

| Allan | I thanked you then and I will thank you now for explaining those tools to me, because all that helped me a lot. I do not want to analyse it too much, it just helps. I do not want to put it any more simply than that. |
| | You do not need to know the whys and wherefores as long as it works for you. It certainly worked for me! |

RELATE AND ASSIMILATE

Allan is a close friend of mine, which is why I was happy to say so much during the interview, and he trusts me, so he just did what I asked him to do, knowing I would only ask him to do things that I would do myself, knowing that I truly believed that what I told him to do would really work, even in his darkest moments.

You can see how he wanted to put things down to luck. This modesty thing we do drives me crazy! This guy is a talented and intelligent man who deserves every bit of his success.

Please, from Allan and me, admit and own up to your power, recognise yourself as 'a mighty one' to quote George Bernard Shaw.

Allan was in a big hole, dice rolled, money blown, huge debts to service, yet he found a way through. He wanted to be 'a millionaire', and if he can do it from where he was financially, then you can certainly do it from where you are.

Write down here, now, three lessons that Allan's story taught you:

1

2

3

'EVERY THOUGHT YOU EVER HAVE'

Mike's Introduction

Wayne was one of our first ever customers, back in 1998 I think we first met. He was a hard sell too, but we got there in the end, and his enthusiasm and persistence have helped us work with thousands of police officers and have a profound effect on their lives and on the lives of people in the communities they serve. None of that would have happened without Big Wayne.

Imagine being crippled with a severe back problem, and having the audacity to dream of regaining so much of your health that you enter Amateur World Championships hoping to win a medal or two.

Well, read about Wayne. Read about Wayne if you are suffering from an illness. Read about Wayne if you think it's too late for you to set out to achieve something. Read about Wayne if an 'expert' has ever told you to forget it.

Wayne uses the tools we share with people as well as anyone I know, and inspires people as much by his example, fire, determination and enthusiasm, as anyone could. I know he will inspire you.

Mike   *So come on Wayne tell everybody the amazing story of how you first came in to contact with us; how did that happen?*

Wayne   Pure chance I think; I'd just got back from Blackburn Police Station where I was working, to the Hutton Hall centre, and I was appointed Acting Chief Inspector for Management Development. I took over an office from my previous incumbent and started going through stacks and stacks of fliers from training suppliers. Sometimes you bin them and sometimes you don't, and I inherited this stack of about 40. So I was going through them and 99% were going in the bin; then I dropped some on the floor by accident, and one caught my eye. I had a quick glance at it and I thought, 'this is different, this is coming at me in a completely different way' and then it was just one of those things, I saw the local telephone number, rather than Manchester or London, and I thought, 'well I should really speak to some companies and find out what's on offer'. So I rang you, and you only live around the corner.

Mike   *Yes and I popped in didn't I?*

Wayne   Yes, you popped in within 24 hours, and I'd already clued up that when these 'reps' come and see you, which effectively you were, try and keep them to half an hour otherwise they'll write your day off! I ended up wanting to keep you there all day, you were that interesting and enthusiastic!

No pessimist ever discovered the secrets of the stars, or sailed to an uncharted land, or opened a new heaven to the human spirit

Helen Keller

Mike   *And then you came on the course with three colleagues.*

Wayne   Yes, the course was brilliant. At the end of the first day I thought it was really powerful. At the end of the second day, when you went round the classroom and asked what we thought, I actually remember being pretty low key about it. I said I liked it, but I was just thinking about it.

I went home, and then something got hold of me. I hardly ever go out running because I've got a bad back, yet I went out for a jog! And it was raining, and it was pretty cold, and it was dark! Still, I went out for this run, and I just thought, 'If I hadn't been on this course, I wouldn't have gone out at all!' It just sort of overwhelmed me, and I kept thinking about it, stronger, stronger, and stronger and I thought, 'next time I see Julie, I have to tell her'. I just had to tell her about it and she couldn't get over it because of how enthusiastic I was.

Then I became renowned at work for talking about this course, and I was just convinced that I had to get it into the organisation. It had so much to offer. Our organisation was going through a massive change process; there was a lot of uncertainty, some dissatisfaction; you know, 'change' doesn't come easily to the Police Service and we could use this - this was the vehicle for taking the change process forward.

Mike   *But hundreds of your people have been through it now, so you were right and people still are coming! You inspired a lot of people.*

Wayne   I like to think I did, and I still do. I talk about it. If there is ever an opportunity, I talk about it. Mike, there was absolutely no way that I could have applied myself to what I have done without living the principles of it; and I have no problem telling people it has changed my life, the quality of my life.

Mike   *Wayne, there are two particularly powerful stories that I always think about when I think about you. One of them was that you had a guy come on the course and he came in to your office and said 'I'm having enormous problems', do you remember this story?*

Wayne   Yes, he thought you had to put 15 minutes aside each day to use the tools you give us, and I just said to him, **'You don't put time aside! It's every thought you ever have!'**

The greatest good you can do for others is not to show your riches, but to reveal to them their own

Benjamin Disraeli

Mike   *The other story, was that there was one woman, and you said to me, 'I've got to get her on the course, her boss tells me about everybody complaining about her attitude!' Do you remember this?*

Wayne   That's right. And basically her manager had said that she was 'unmanageable' and 'we can't do anything with her!'

The course was mentioned, and he said, 'well if you can change her with that, then I wouldn't believe it!' So she came in to see me, and she said, 'they're going to put me down for this course because they think I'm negative', and I said what it had done for me and I think we talked for about half an hour. At the end of the half hour she was really buzzing with it and she agreed to go on to the course!

We booked her in for a couple of weeks ahead, and before she even went on the course, her manager came to me and said, 'what have you done with Margaret? She is brilliant!'

He said, 'it's the first ever time we've known, that the prospect of going on a course has changed someone, never mind actually attending it!'

Mike   *You phoned me after you had that word with him and said, 'you are not going to believe this!'*

Wayne   Yes, and when she went on the course she absolutely loved it and now she is Secretary to the Chief Superintendent!

Mike   *These things which I think about with you show me the impact that you've had not only on yourself but on other people with it, you know, you talk about young Shaun and his Basketball and Rowing, and you have used it in so many areas of your life, especially during the problems with your health; tell us about that.*

137

Wayne	Well I have always had a sporting background, from being 16 when I was a bit of a runner and 20 when I won the UK Open National Wrestling Championship.

I've also played Basketball for twenty odd years and it was always my intention that I'd still be playing for the Police Athletics Association, PAA Basketball, the year I retire.

I have played with a bad back for years and years, it was kind of almost hereditary, all my brothers and sisters and my mum and dad have got bad backs.

About eight years ago I had a very bad disc problem – caused by a sneeze! I was off work for eight months and had the disc out of my back. I then came back to fitness with a vengeance, determined that I would do things. I continued to play basketball and volleyball for the Police, took up the Triathlon, and still played football in the summer and stuff like that, but I just enjoyed my sport that much, that I just wanted to keep going and doing something.

Over the last number of years, playing volleyball and basketball, my back was getting more and more sore; I'd had other back problems that were related and so eventually, I was taken for a second back operation. I remember being in hospital, and the nurse came to me and said, 'you are just going to have to be really careful; you really must slow down; you can't keep doing these things; you've just got to take it easy'.

I gained a stone in weight, yet tried playing basketball and volleyball again. Of course my back got sore again, so then I took my time with Julie to lose some weight and half way through the programme I joined the gym again. I lost 30 pounds, which I was really pleased with, and found myself on the rowing machine getting more enjoyment out of that than being on the bike.

I had dabbled in rowing years ago, when I just went at it like a mad man and it made my back sore, so I never touched it again. That was about 12 years ago and I thought, 'I'm really enjoying this'.

Then I had two or three months where I started doing long rows and remembering my times and how far I could row in 20 minutes, and the test for any rower relates entirely to Olympic Rowing, which is 2000 metres – the machine was designed to train Olympic Rowers – the amount of effort required to row 2000 metres on this machine is basically the same as it is to row in the water.

I had a go and it took me just under 8 minutes (7 minutes 52 seconds) and I wrote it down and I got the 'Concept 2' magazine, and in there was the age rankings for thousands of people in the UK. Every gym has got one of these machines, and I looked up my age in the chart for 40-50 years olds, 2000 metres, and it put me 388th in the United Kingdom. So I thought, 'right, I know how fit I am compared to that, so what I'll do is I'll start training and I'll get better'.

So I've given up team sport effectively and I've given up basketball/volleyball, and I said to myself, 'this is for me this, for me to measure how good I am, and how hard I can train.' My back was really good; I'd had no problems, which was probably because I had just started steadily, so I set out myself a training log.

Every couple of months I had a go at my PB, (personal best), and always got it and then I'd try 500 metres, 1000 metres and then 2000 metres and I just kept doing it and getting better and better. Then, about Summer last year, there was a competition at the YMCA, where I train, for a 2000 metre row, so I set myself a target of winning the competition.

They had age categories and there were some really fit lads there, but I decided what I would do was win the competition, but not win the 40-50 year category, but the 20 and 30 year olds, I would beat them, and there were some ripping young lads there who were doing all right.

Anyway, I won the whole competition! And now I was rising up through the ranks from 388th, and I was getting certainly into the top 100 in the UK. So then I thought I would enter the National Championships in Reading in November and I thought this is another competition and this is what I am going to do - I'm going to go there and compare myself to the best in the country.

I really did set about my training with a vengeance. I was training really hard for the YMCA competition and pushed myself to the extreme really and I just kept improving. Every time you sit on the machine, you've got to be so strong mentally, that's how Redgrave has done it; he has just had the mental ability to apply himself over twenty years. It is such a mental thing, because the effort required is massive, it really is, and I've just been applying myself through positive thinking to achieve and to never stop improving.

I have never stopped improving yet and every page of my 50

page training log has yellow highlighter pen on it, and yellow highlighter pen means a personal best in something, be it 300 metres or an hour's row. Every page has got something that I've never done better before, and when I sit on the machine and go for a personal best it happens. I mean I scare myself some days in that I can just keep improving, and I've spoken to people in the know, and asked them, 'how good can I get?' and they say, 'well you're not there yet because you, effectively, have only been training hard for just over a year.'

When I went to Reading, I registered with a personal best of six minutes 38 seconds and that ranked me 10th, and it was overwhelming. I'd always imagined – I never wrote an 'ID' down about what I was going to do – but I was always on the rostrum in my mind, and the thought of going out and not winning a medal there, never entered my head.

Mike   *You phoned me the day before you left didn't you?*

Wayne   Well actually, I phoned you just after Dublin, where I entered the Dublin Open, because I didn't feel strong, and I did record a personal best by 0.4 of a second even though I felt rubbish.

So I phoned you up after that because I was worried, but also I was thinking if I feel rubbish I won't achieve my personal best at Reading, and you certainly helped me with that one, in that you said, 'Wayne, if that's how good you are when you don't feel well, just imagine how good you will be when you are well!' That just gave me a bit more confidence and made me relax a bit more.

So when I got to Reading, everything was right; the warm up, the preparation on the day, my wife and lad were there, and you just think, 'this is it; this is a year of torture and it's going to mean something to me this! I am getting onto that rostrum!'

And six and a half minutes went and I have maybe four memories of it – I heard my name mentioned at the beginning, and I'm looking at this dial that shows these numbers, and I only have to move my eyes half an inch and I can see Julie and Shaun, because they are sat directly opposite in the back seating, yet I never even saw them – and they screamed their heads off and I never heard anything, and Julie took about six photos of me, and said I looked like I was possessed; and I do look like I was possessed, my eyes are bulging, and it hurt a lot.

At the end I fell off the machine, and I had broken my personal best by five whole seconds. I was ranked 10th at half way, and rowed the quickest second half of the race of anyone in the field!

That was just the greatest sporting moment of my life really and I just felt, 'no one can take this away from you now, you've done it', and almost immediately I was so emotional; and after it I could not believe it.

From losing a bit of weight, being nearly 400th in the UK, to gaining a bronze medal in less than a year and I've got that now for life!

And the stupid thing is that Doctors and people who have had back operations wouldn't recommend a rowing machine if you've got a bad back and that's probably sound advice; it can cause back problems, but for some reason it has suited me and I'm bloody good at it now to say the least.

Following Reading I set my target – I wanted to do The World Police and Fire Games coming up this summer, which is a big competition. Just by pure chance I was in the training centre and there was a thick brochure that came through for New Zealand, The World Service Games – it was obviously posted out from New Zealand to every Constabulary, Fire Brigade, Army Headquarters, Navy, Air Force, Customs, and Prison organisation in the world and I just read it and thought, 'yes, this is the next step.'

I went home and showed it to Julie and she was brilliant; she just said, 'if you want to go, and that's what you want to do, just do it. If that will quench your thirst, then do it.' So I wrote off and applied and booked my flight and then something else really spooky happened.

On the Tuesday I was due to row at New Zealand I had a 10 year endowment mature on that day, which paid for the whole trip! It paid for that one and the Police and Fire Games in Indianapolis – it paid for both trips, and Julie and Shaun are coming out with me! So something I had taken out ten years ago just matured on that day, and I had forgotten all about it, didn't even remember it! It's almost as if that was how it was meant to happen.

Mike   *So you popped in here just before you shot off to New Zealand.*

Wayne   I just needed a top up, yes, because now this was the world stage. As I remember it, when we did speak I probably did most of the talking, probably because I was that fired up about it! I was looking to you to agree with me; and how I had got my mind set right and you did that and more, so I felt pretty damned confident.

When I was speaking to you and other people as well, I always said, 'I'll do good, I must be up there; I must be in with a shout for the medals,' and I always said, 'as long as I keep healthy; as long as I keep well,' because it was a long flight, it's like two days in the air. You set off Thursday morning from Manchester and arrive Saturday morning in Christchurch. That must have been preying on my mind.

So I arrived there Saturday lunch and I'm rowing on the Monday lunch so it's not ideal preparation with the jet lag. Within six hours of landing I got a sore throat and then that night it was like swallowing broken glass and so Sunday morning I'm starting to dose myself up with Vitamin C and cold remedies and stuff like that and I'm frightened to death of not feeling well the next day.

Monday morning comes and I'm not feeling well and my limbs are aching, I'm sweating, my throat's terrible and I just start with a tickly cough.

Mike   And how much of that was mental, do you think?

Wayne   Let's just say I wish I'd never said, 'as long as I keep healthy!' You did tell me that the subconscious mind is ALWAYS listening! I know it made sure that I didn't feel well!

So when I sat on the machine and did the warm up, a couple of thousand metres, and one or two five-second blasts flat out, 'it' was there! When I hit the machine, it read what I wanted it to read.

At the machines, they had a big screen with little digital boats so you can watch the others.

Now, because the first event was to be my first ever 2000 metre individual, I didn't want to push it too much; I didn't want to blow up, because I didn't know, although I could pull hard, I didn't know how fit I'd be for the full 2000 metres, and didn't know whether I would just fade or whatever.

So I thought I'd go out hard, see where I am in the field – I rowed in my glasses for the first time so I could see what the digital boats were saying! – went out really hard for 500 metres, and thought, 'well I'm up there! I'm in the lead!' and thought, 'I'll just hold it!' and I held it, and kind of eased off just marginally in the middle, and I felt good, so I pushed the last 500 and I came off the machine not dead, and rowed 6 minutes 34.1 seconds, which is a second outside the personal best which I'd set at Reading, but when I sat on the machine that day in New Zealand, I wasn't going to row for me, I was going to row to win.

It was about winning and I won. I was within a second of a PB, and I thought, 'you're good here!' and then before my next race, which was in less than an hour's time, the 500 metres individual, the New Zealand captain came up to me, a Maori – smashing bloke – we shook hands and he said, 'how do you fancy rowing in the pairs in my age category, the Masters?' It was 10 years below me, so he was in age category 35-44, and he was 39, but he was a top class rower, and I said yes!

I felt a bit rough but I thought, 'I've come all this way, I've got the opportunity of doing two more rows, I've won one and they can't take that away from me,' plus the fact that the next event was only going to be a short row, and it was only going to last a minute and a half! So I thought, 'I'll do that!'

So I rowed in the 500 and just blasted it and went out for a personal best and got 0.9 of a second off my personal best, which is like another four metres in the water, so I had just shattered that and I just felt tremendous then.

Then I rowed in the pairs with him; rowed next to him and he's experienced and he just talked me through it. It was really good because as we sat next to each other, I rowed the same lengths as him, so our seats were coming backwards and forwards at the same time, so I matched his rate.

He was pulling slightly harder than I was and it felt great! The 2000 metres just went in no time at all, and we were confident that we had won – and we did! Three Gold Medals on the first day!

I went home, had a nice big tea, just one beer, and then next day I had so much confidence because basically the same rowers were rowing in all three events, so I sat on the machine and thought, 'I'm just going to go for it as fast as I can. I'm going to get my personal best,' and I did! 1.4 seconds inside my personal best and I was in a really bad way afterwards! I had given everything!

Luckily you can recover very quickly from that, but the one thousand metres is different. I rowed really strong and won that and then a couple of hours later we rowed in the 1000 pairs and we won that too! **Five Golds out of five!**

Mike   *That took Sir Steven Redgrave sixteen years!*

Wayne   Don't mention my name in the same breath as his! He's an icon. But I have had a taste of how hard someone like Redgrave would have to train. I've done it as an amateur, trained twice a day so I'm as committed as I can be, holding down a full time job, but then to put yourself through it for 20 years - it's a different level; but I think I know how he feels because I'm sure it hurts me just as much when I train as it does him. It was fantastic.

Mike   *When we heard, we were just so delighted for you, if you can imagine, we were just all jumping up and down!*

Wayne   I talked about you to the Maori lad; he was interested in it so you got it to the other side of the world on that day, because he couldn't get over the fact that when I sit down to row a personal best, that's what I do!

Mike   *Incredible.*

Wayne   And I make sure now I never say 'I'll never ever get to that level'. I don't entertain thoughts that I could ever row as fast as Redgrave, but then I don't know what Redgrave will be rowing when he's 45, so who knows eh? He might not even be rowing, in which case, I'll be alright!

Mike   *That story is an inspirational story and you are an inspirational person; what would you say to people who are facing a challenge in their lives now, maybe like the one you had, maybe something different?*

Wayne   I would say, 'how would you like your life to be? What is success to you?' I've used your course to change my life; there is never an hour goes by when I don't think about trying to be positive with everything. I'd also say, don't limit yourself! Don't let other people limit you! Just do what you can, and live it and it will happen, because it has happened to me, because that's what I wanted.

Mike   *You've made it happen, I came to visit you in hospital and I saw you and you couldn't even move and it's amazing to think what can be done isn't it?*

Wayne   I was on the touch line watching Rugby on Sunday and I was speaking to my Doctor, who is a friend of yours, Tim, who was the Bolton Wanderers Doctor, and he said, 'oh, I've heard you've done brilliantly'. I was speaking to him before I went, and he couldn't get over what I had done especially with my bad back.

Mike   *But you've inspired him because you've inspired everyone, I mean you inspire people.*

Wayne   People know that they cannot come in to my office and talk negatively! We once did this promotion, where we were going to sell a leadership course to local businesses, and these local business people turned up, and we put on a display and gave a talk. It was a partnership initiative with a training company, and at the end of all this, we had used quite a lot of resource to put this on, but no one wanted it; we'd got it all wrong – marketing wise got it all wrong!

Then we were going to have a meeting with the Head of Training and before the meeting, we laid down the ground rules. We were going to have a de-brief of the project, and basically I said, 'I will not allow a negative thing to be said about it. There will be no blame on anybody here.

What we are going to do is find out where we went wrong.....

Find out where we could have done it better, but no one will attach any blame to any one person, or else the team is walking out.'

Previously, we would have had an hour of bashing everything and everybody! But team members came out and said, 'I cannot believe how well that meeting went.' I mean we got it wrong, but there were so many positives that came out that people were just amazed at the end of it.

Mike   *Now that's how you run a meeting, a team, a business, and a life!*

RELATE AND ASSIMILATE

Wayne has rediscovered something he seemed to have lost when I first met him

- a lust for life, and a belief that all things are possible. He also taught me that nothing can stand in the way of desire, belief and determination. Nothing.

He has just returned from the World Games in the USA, and I have already heard that he came back with at least one more Gold Medal.

Wayne is never happy to rest on his laurels, he also knows that 'the race is long, and in the end it's only with yourself', and so he pushes himself to beat himself, because Wayne has shown me, that that is where the real Gold is.

What did you learn from Wayne?

1

2

3

'JUST GIVE ME THE TOOLS!'

Mike's Introduction

I first met Ros when I called to see her boss, and remember how confident and in control she seemed. The reality was somewhat different. She tells in her story that she had been desperately ill for many years, and that simply making it through a day was impossible, never mind coming on a strange training course!

She tells how nervous she was, but how, after years of searching, she quickly realised that she had found the answer to her troubles. Andrew fondly recalls how, after only a couple of hours, Ros was completely sold, and became so impatient to get to the end of the course so that she could get out there and change her life!

This woman has changed her life using what she describes as 'simple' techniques, and now throws down the gauntlet to every one of us to do the same.

Mike	*So come on Ros, it's not that long since you and I first met properly, and you went on the course with Andrew about a year ago. What happened?*
Ros	I actually went on the course because my old boss from work said that he thought that I might find some benefit from it. At that point I wasn't working there. I had become ill in the July. A friend of mine had gone on the course around Christmas time and said, 'Look Ros go on it! I am not going to tell you what it is about, just go on it, but I think it's wonderful!'
	So I thought, well if my friend says that and my boss says that, then I'll trust them and I will go with them and go on the course. So I got a date sorted out. I was a bit nervous because I had not gone on something like that for a quite a long time.
	I knew nothing about it when I arrived, and I felt the whole experience deeply because I was still quite ill, and I found some situations a bit difficult because I was scared that I would not be able to handle a full day.
Mike	*And you didn't know anybody on the course either!*
Ros	No, but it was important to me that I went there, anonymously, because I was going for my own personal thing. So I got a date, and, about a week before, I was fuelling myself about the course and saying 'You have got to make sure that you eat so that you can go through the course'. I was kind of excited but restless. But I was saying, 'Yes, I can do this'. So I think the

course was the Thursday and Friday. The Thursday came, I set my alarm and at that time I used to get up as and when, and I was not used to my alarm going off.

I had to make sure I got there on time as I have a habit of usually being late.

I think I was a little bit late. I kind of walked into the room and thought, 'Well, I'm here now.' I had a look around the room and saw all the people. I think I was quite quiet for the first few hours. But I think right from the start my attention was grabbed. I just found that what Andrew was saying was really interesting. I had been on another course like this by a very well known person before and I was scared that it was going to be something like that.

I think that because of the way Andrew did the course and the way he was, he was saying, 'I am not saying that every day will be fantastic or that it will be wonderful; you will have bad days, but it will kind of help you'.

I must have kept saying to him, 'I want the tools now!' I was so intrigued and wowed, even after just a couple of hours!

What stuck in my head was, **that if you have the goals and the belief and the desire then it's yours.**

I remember thinking, 'Why do people tell me all the time, 'You can't, you aren't capable!', and I think that is the kind of thing that I took, that stayed with me.

Since the course, I have found that I now have the belief in myself and it does not matter what people say. If I believe in it and I want it, then I am going to have it and I can do it, and so I no longer care what people think. The course taught me that I have the right to do that.

I think that if the course had been any sooner I would not have been ready to take all that on board. It came at the right time.

It was what I was waiting for.

I think that when I first booked the course, Personnel said the date was around December, and I said, 'No, I will go to the one in February', so I think now that it must have been a subconscious thing, deciding to go then.

Mike   *It's almost as if people know when the time is right for them. We really do need to listen to and trust our subconscious more!*

Ros	So anyway, on the course lots of talk went on with the other people, and we were quite a close group, and I think the third day, a couple of months later, was the closest of all. There were people there who had been on the first two days, where I think work had put them through, and they were just kind of, you know, 'I've heard it all before', they were sceptical, and it spoilt it in a way because most of us were really excited.

But by the third day it was amazing how they had ALL changed! The people I had met on the two-day course, in a way, we kind of touched lives. You do not often meet people like that, but they touched my life maybe only briefly but it had an effect on my life.

It was all very well explained, by Andrew, because I like things to be simple; the simpler they are, the better I can understand them. And because it was mixed in with the offers to talk to others who have done all this, who will help you, you just had to sit up and listen. And boy, did I want to get those tools!

I imagined a toolkit, a little box with spanners and things, which I would go off with!

At the end of Day One I was absolutely shattered. I went home and put on the answer machine and I thought I am not speaking to anybody tonight. I pulled the curtains and jumped in the bath and went to bed about 8 o'clock! I wanted to collect what I had heard, mull it over. I was keen to go back because I wanted to get those tools!

I could not wait for the second day to come!

On the second day the whole group was much more of a group really, and I think I felt more comfortable, and I had made a friendship with these two girls from Liverpool.

I actually felt like 'a chosen one', that we'd been picked to go on this workshop and we had been given a wonderful thing.

Then I suppose I felt like an 'Ambassador'! I used to go round and tell people (it was quite funny sometimes, you know!) about this course and the one thing after the course was that I didn't have time for half-hearted people that were like, 'Oh, I can't do a lot'. I felt like saying, 'Oh for goodness sake! **YOU CAN CHANGE IT, BECAUSE I CAN!**'

Mike	*Would you not have recognised that so much had you not done the course?*

Ros	No I think I would have been saying, 'Oh what a shame!' and making it worse for them!

But now I am finding that my tolerance has changed. I have looked at the people that are there in my life and that I want to share things with, and the 'down people', who say 'You can't do it; you can't be rich or whatever', and have just thought, 'I do not need to hear that from you anymore!' I just wanted to be around people who were positive. It's true that if the people you do see are miserable, then it makes you miserable. I just don't want them around because they do not help.

The other thing that amazed me about the course was that when we got the tool kit, I couldn't believe how simple it was!

With the other course I mentioned earlier, you had to lie down, play the tape and it wasn't practical.

But then here was the tool kit and it was simple. It was so simple that I thought, 'I can do this'. I think these two girls and I, we all said between us that when we came back, as they were coming back on the third day, the same day as me, that we would all make a goal which we would come back with.

So mine was that I would get my business cards done. One of the girls was going to have decorated her bedroom, something that had been annoying her for years but that was quite simple; and the other girl I think was going to do something to do with her job. We said we would come back in March and we were going to have done these things. I wanted to test these simple things out.

My first simple little test was, I used to bite my nails and my nails used to be absolutely awful. They were bitten right down there and I hated them. So I went home and thought, 'Right!' It was a simple test, and one that I could see results from.

So I got a piece of paper and I wrote on it, I still have the card somewhere, 'I have beautiful nails that I can now paint the colour to go with my outfit'. Of course I had a picture in my head of these wonderful nails that I had.

I think at the time that I used to pick up the cards and take them back into the bathroom, so that when I was in the bath I could see what I was thinking about. Anyway I just pictured this in my head and then suddenly, I was not even aware that I had stopped! I just did not bite them anymore and suddenly my nails were growing.

I went back for the third day of the course, and turned up with these wonderful nails and of course my business cards. I had really bugged my Dad, saying, 'Look Dad, I have to take this card with me and I don't care if it's not quite finished, but I just have to take this card.' If I hadn't done I would have been so upset because I had to do it.

So that got me going on the business side of things, and the third thing I had wanted which I have not said previously, was about my illness.

But the simple tests that I succeeded with, to me were just so simple, and gave me such belief then that I could do anything.

I found that I was more of a visual person, so although I did write my goals down as Andrew taught us to, it was the picture in my head to me that lasted longer. I suppose that in my subconscious I no longer bite my nails, and I have beautiful nails, but I did not actually sit there every morning and read the card.

So it was so easy, it was not difficult at all, and I just felt so positive, and I suppose that I felt that it was the right time, and something clicked and I just felt like a different person.

But I suppose that the way that it really helped me, and it's a long story, was with my illness. I was 16 or 17 when I first started suffering with anorexia. I would never admit that I had a problem and I would not allow myself to be aware and I completely denied the whole thing.

But it was July, two years ago, when I collapsed at work but I got myself into this state where I had given up I suppose.

I just wasn't happy and I collapsed at work and I was off work sick and my days were spent just kind of mulling around the house. I wasn't capable of doing a lot because I was so pathetic. I couldn't move, or couldn't lift things. It was quite awful.

I entered this world of anorexia and I got with people who were anorexic and it was kind of a world in a bubble really. I would potter around the house. I would not bother getting dressed.

At first when I first went to the clinic I was quite scared about the whole thing and I thought, 'I am never going to get better' and 'how can I get better'. Then I just thought 'You will get better' but I never really believed it.

Things carried on from the July until Christmas and I think I had lost a bit more weight and I had started doing a course at college, which I enjoyed although I found quite difficult. I got help from the clinic but then again, it was quite difficult having therapy and all that kind of thing.

I think it was on New Year's day and my boyfriend came round and he said, 'Look Ros, you are getting no better. I have seen no improvement, and it's about time you did something and got yourself out of this rut.' It was a real good shake and that is why I think that the course when it came up was at the right time.

He said, 'Look Ros, either do something about it all or just do not even bother to talk about it.' Although it was a very hard thing for him to do, it worked.

I suppose the course helped in so many ways that it is hard to explain, but it just gave me this inner belief that I am a lovely person and that I am worth being me and I have nothing to be ashamed of and that I can be me and I just suddenly got the will to get better and I just wanted to live again.

I remember I wrote, I might have it here actually on this piece of paper, and it is called 'My Promise' and it says 'I will be true to myself. I don't need people's approval. I am responsible for what I want to do. I am going to do what I want to do, and I love me and I am worth the same as **anybody**.'

Mike	*Did you write that during the course?*
Ros	Yes, I had it pinned on my notice board so that every morning 'My Promise' was there. And I think that just writing that was just enough in itself, in that it kind of gave an affirmation to me that I do love me and it does not matter what other people think or how they think. I love me and what I do I am doing for me.
Mike	*Are you saying that a lot of things that were going on in your life were making you hate yourself or making you negative about yourself at the time?*
Ros	I suppose so, yes.
Mike	*I am just trying to get at why it was so important to you to write that promise. A lot of people could do with doing that.*
Ros	I tried to please people. I was a bit of a door mat; my self confidence was at rock bottom. I did not think highly of myself.

I suppose I became this person, who just gave everything to everybody else and forgot about me and what I want.

Mike   *A lot of people do that, don't they? That is such a powerful thing to say here because lots of people need to hear that message about themselves; that they are important. That is not a sinful thing to say at all, yet sometimes people are made to feel as if it is!*

Ros   I think the course taught me, 'believe in yourself because if you do not then nobody else will'. So it was like somebody saying that of course you can think that; why would you not think that!

But because Andrew told me that I could believe in myself, although I know I should not have had to be told that, I said, 'okay, yes I can'.

So I started to accept *me* more and, with leaving work and starting my own business, people around me were saying, 'Well you are stupid. You are leaving a job that you have been in for quite a few years; it is good money, and it is a good job.' And I was saying, 'I do not want to do it, I know what I want to do, this is what I want'.

They would say, 'You won't have any money,' so I would say, 'Well, I don't care, I am doing it.' I didn't want to say look, you know, 'I will prove it', because I was not proving it to anybody. I was doing it because I wanted to do it but a lot of people thought I was stupid, but then there were others who helped me and said 'Go on, go for it, do you want any help?' and that was wonderful. That did hurt me, especially my Mum, who was one of the people who said, 'I don't think you should.'

Mike   *They are frightened of you failing, aren't they?*

Ros   I think it was like they were trying to protect me, because I was starting to get better, and it might be too much for me, and I was saying 'No Mum!', and I stood by it all along. I kept saying, 'I don't know how, I don't know when, but it is going to happen, it is going to work, so just believe me'.

I think people have seen the change in me, in that I have accomplished so much in one year, and I want to say to people, 'Look, you can do it as well, I am not special. Just do it'.

It helped me accept the person that I am and that I was and what I wanted to do and that I should believe in myself, but the other thing is me getting better and putting on weight.

So, after the course, I said 'I have got a problem'. I hadn't told people on the course; I didn't want to be this anorexic person, I wanted to go as me. So, after the course I accepted that I did have a problem and I set myself a target weight, for I think it was my birthday - 7½ stone by 16th June. Now I felt at this point that, 'if you don't meet it, it doesn't matter, don't beat yourself up, but that is the goal that you are going to go for.' I thought that was one that was achievable, so I wrote it down in my little book, 'target weight 7½ stone'.

I used to go to the clinic to be weighed every four weeks and of course every time I went I would write the date and the weight I was. I went on the course in February, and the third day of the course was in March. I went to the clinic; I think it was a day prior to the course and that was when I shared with the group what had happened.

I had just found out the day before that I had put on half a kilogramme. It was not a lot, but the biggest thing was that I was actually pleased about it. Previously I would have either lost weight or put it back on to be level again or it hadn't changed.

Somehow I had put on half a kilo and I was so happy.

I just thought I just had to tell them. I felt so pleased. And part of me felt, 'I don't want them to think of me as this anorexic girl', but I thought, 'No, I want to share it' and when it came to my turn to share what we had been up to, I started off with the nails and then the business cards and then I came out with this.

I knew that I was going to cry because I felt so relaxed, but I just wanted to say it. I just felt so proud of myself and so pleased that I had just turned a corner and I think that sharing it with the group made me want to get better even more.

So something just happened between me going on this course and the third day; it had completely turned around. I think as well that I have in my head a picture of me and I can't describe the picture. It is a picture in my head, which I cannot transfer. It is just a picture of me, happy, healthy; I have a picture of what I have got on, what the weather is like and I just have this picture. I have this picture and that is how I am going to be.

I try to explain it to people and I say, 'Look, I have this picture of me and this is how I am going to be, I can't explain it, but I know I am going to get better, so watch me!'

So, I am going back to the clinic every four weeks and I get weighed, and each week I have been putting on and putting on weight. I came to the 16th June and I think I was one pound off my 7½ stone!

Starting in February at 6½ stone, I am just looking in my book, yes I started on 3rd February at 44.7 kg, then by 16th March my weight had gone up to 45.5; so in between the first two days of the course and the third day I had put on probably just over ½ kg. After that it went up to 46.6 kg, 47.2, 48.9, 49.6, and 50.8 kg by September. I had gone up by 6 kg almost.

I gave myself the next target after June to be eight stone sometime around September and that was a bit of a landmark because to me eight stone feels a lot.

I have a picture in my head about how you see your life in five years' time. I did it not really thinking about it, I just wrote it and I read it about two weeks ago and it has actually come true. It is amazing.

In the letter I put things about a new house, just decorated; things about my boyfriend, that are fantastic. The aromatherapy is wonderful, business is picking up. The thing that hadn't happened was that I had fallen pregnant, but something that did happen was that I had gone about two years without a period, and that actually came back the day I moved into the new house.

So just by writing it down it happened, just because I have written them down and visualised them in my head. I do not know how, where or when, but it just happens.

I just know this person two or three years ago would never have thought it possible, but it is because of your course that this happens - okay it is me as well, but it is because of what you have shown me that my whole life has turned around. I am so proud of myself and I feel so much a stronger person for it.

Mike   *No-one is going to get in your way; no-one is going to stop you and you have your whole life in front of you!*

Ros   Yes, I am now recovering, I have my own business, and my personal life with my partner is so much better; it is unbelievable. I just feel so content.

Mike   *How does he feel now, looking back at you on that New Year's Day and looking at you now?*

Ros   He said to me, 'I have done nothing for you, you have done all

155

this by yourself, I am very proud of you because I have done nothing'. And I say, 'Yes, but you have been there for me, you have listened when I have maybe had a tearful outburst or you have been there for me to share things with, you have done a lot.'

In some way I think he is almost jealous – not in a nasty way but I think he feels that this is a fantastic person and feels, 'So, why don't I change my life?'

Mike   *You were probably easier to live with before!*

Ros   Yes, but I think he probably is amazed and I think he knows now that if I say I am going to do it, it damn well gets done. I mean it is like moving into this house; I set myself a target that within the first two weeks that I would have all the boxes unpacked and all the rooms decorated. Saturday, a day early, I painted the bedroom, my treatment room, painted the kitchen, and stripped and painted the dining room, and it was all done. Everything was done. I just cannot be bothered messing around now.

Mike   *This is a girl who a year ago couldn't move!*

Ros   Yes, going into town to do a bit of shopping, was like a mammoth expedition! I'd get panic attacks, my limbs would ache and I would get tired.

I have talked to my Dad about it as well because he was always so negative, and everything was rubbish and I said, 'I have been on this course and it is nothing spectacular but look it works. If you want I will talk to you about it. But it's so simple.'

I think I said that if you were having a really bad day think of one thing that has happened that is good and focus on that and try to be a bit more positive (you have to be careful not to say the wrong thing so as not to upset him!)

He has been seeing me for aromatherapy treatment, and because he has seen a change in me and how I have changed, he has become a different person! I think he should come on this course. I think he would get so much out of it as well. He has read loads of books on positive thinking.

If anyone asked me 'what is the best thing that you have ever been offered,' I would say your training programme.

Mike   *So the reality is, that there are millions of people who put everybody before themselves and they do not value themselves. They need to do something, they need their proverbial kick or whatever, and it may be that some of them need to come on this course. What would you say to them?*

Ros   I would say...I would probably say quite a lot, but it would probably be something like, 'don't waste your life because it's your life, grab it, do it (it is hard to put it into words) it is so easy to do it, don't waste any more time, if you want to do it just do it and never look back and you will think when you have done it, 'why did I not do it sooner?' Go for it and do it. It is so easy.'

I do not think I have done anything special; I have just got on with life.

Anybody can do it. **If I can, then anybody can**, because I am not special, but I decided that if I want to change things, then only I can change it.

RELATE AND ASSIMILATE

Well, at one point I felt a little tear during that interview, as Ros built a picture of her life and her illness, and as she explained how SHE turned it around.

She has taught me that if she can turn her life around, then you can do it too.

She has taught me the power of setting believable goals, and the meaning of small steps that feel like giant leaps.

Let's all just take her advice and get on with it!

What did you learn?

1

2

3

'How long could it take to build a Rolls Royce Aero Engine?'

Mike's Introduction

Tony Burns is a ball of fire; a blur of energy, enthusiasm and creativity, as you'll see. His personal story is also a corporate one of teamwork and visionary leadership in a world class business. Tony talks about reducing the build time for an engine from 400 days, down to 40, to 27, even down as low as 20, based on an initial discussion around whether even 10 might be possible. The implications for what Tony tells us are extraordinary, involving savings of hundreds of millions of pounds! Wow is this stuff powerful!

Tony's Story

This is a story about how an organisation's limiting belief was challenged and finally changed through the power of an "inevitable dream" plus a whole lot of astounding teamwork following an incredible workshop arranged by our visionary boss Trevor Orman, and run by Michael Finnigan.

Out of that course was born the "40-Day Engine" challenge - to procure, build, assemble and test a complete Trent aero-engine within 40 calendar days by the end of 2003.

If successful, it would radically transform the amount of inventory that the Company held in engine parts and free up working capital to be better used in investing for the future in new product development and facilities - exactly what was needed to deliver the growth in demand for Rolls-Royce's products into the new millennium.

The scale of the challenge was huge - the existing time to complete the engines at that time was over 10 times the proposed 40 calendar days. You can no doubt guess how these targets were regarded by team members and managers within the build and test areas!

I was asked to become the 40-Day Champion for the Civil Aerospace business.

In the early days, most of my time and effort was spent on communicating the purpose and goals of the Project. Well, if I'm honest that's not entirely true. Due to the fact that most of the line managers in the business felt that they had not been consulted in the target setting stage (true), there was almost institutional resistance towards the development of any plans towards achieving the goal. But more than the feeling of having been left out of the target setting, I believe that the main reason for the resistance was a genuine belief that the originally discussed ten day goal was beyond the capability of the operation. **A limiting belief pervaded the organisation and again, being honest, I too was in that camp.**

Then, suddenly and tragically, the September 11th attacks occurred and things changed. Within a very short space of time the aerospace market found itself in a tail-spin as airlines started to defer aircraft and engine orders as consumer confidence eroded in the short-term. Rolls-Royce found itself having to drastically re-shape its production programmes which in turn resulted in work-force redundancies. The underlying goal of the "40-Day Engine" was about reducing lead-times and increasing responsiveness – exactly what Rolls-Royce needed during these critical times if it was to survive and prosper.

Something else changed during the last few months of 2001; Trevor Orman was appointed as Operations Director for the Civil Aerospace business. Trevor had been recruited from outside of Rolls-Royce and brought with him much experience from his time within General Motors, where he had been responsible for running production facilities plus successfully driving large change programmes. The original recruitment brief had been focussed on how to change the business to meet the growing needs of the Rolls-Royce order book. By the time he had taken up the appointment, he was overseeing a downsizing exercise. I mention this as it might explain why the idea of a 10-Day engine still did not seem to me to be as high on the priority list of the leadership team as I thought it should be. I still could not see a plan that would get us to our target on time and did start to feel that my efforts were becoming pointless.

It was towards the end of 2002 that Trevor established his Business Transformation Team – "The BTT". I was fortunate to be selected as one of the original members along with Ian Hill, "Spike" Johnston, Nick Hill and Eibhlin Halpin. Trevor had by now formulated his strategic vision for the business – to Aspire to World Class. It would require lots of change - in its plant, its processes and its people - and we were the team that would help enable it. We were his "Fix It Team". In some instances we were also the "Break it first then Fix It Team"! Trevor explained to us what he wanted us to do and then let us get on with it – he had confidence in us and believed we would deliver. It was infectious, because we also believed that we would deliver and invariably we did.

It was now mid 2003 and despite the amount of progress we were making in changing the processes, our headline performance measure of engine lead-time remained stubbornly high. There was immense pressure on the business to improve performance and to do it quickly. We were also not being helped by a poorly performing supply chain that was itself still coming to terms with life after September 11th. Late delivery of parts to the assembly shop was a daily occurrence that had to be managed and it was extremely disruptive. The 2003 year-end target of 10 days was now looming as a serious embarrassment for the business – whilst perversely providing a rich source of self-justification for those who had stated from the outset that "it was impossible".

Now, remember that Mike Finnigan had been introduced to Trevor's first line management team when he delivered the "impossible goals to inevitable dreams" training course as part of the leadership development programme within the business. The effects of this course were ultimately to become quite significant in the following few years within the business, but the immediate effect was quite simple and very dramatic, as this story will show. Trevor wanted to make a breakthrough on engine lead-time performance before year-end and established an "inevitable dream" to achieve a 20 day engine. This wasn't as challenging as the original 10 day engine goal, but it still represented a significant improvement whilst being more realistic – a smarter goal. He realised that we would not have the processes in place to deliver 20 days consistently – this would require the advent of the flow-lines in 2004 – but he just needed to establish a new "best performance" that would inspire people and be the benchmark for his World Class vision. It would enable the organisation to share his "inevitable dream".

Ian Hill had taken over the leadership of the BTT and had been on the same training course that had inspired Trevor to set the "inevitable dream". He too had been inspired and bought into the dream. As I was still acting as 40-Day Engine Champion for the business, he wanted me to lead the task of trying for the 20 Day engine so he set about trying to inspire me; sharing the vision of the inevitable dream. Whilst I originally still had some doubts about the organisation's ability to deliver, I was quick to pick up on Ian's belief that the task was possible and I understood the benefit that this would have towards the longer term aims of the business. The "inevitable dream" was starting to form in my mind too.

We needed the cooperation of the team members who were building the engine so we set about sharing our "inevitable dream" with them. At a series of team meetings prior to the launch of the engine, we communicated our goals, rationale and requirements of them. Whilst it was new information for most of the team members, repeating the message served as "self-talk" for Ian and I and reinforced our vision of success.

There was some resistance in parts, but on the whole the teams were very supportive of what we were doing. There was though a general feeling of desperation that they were not able to perform at their best through limitations put on them by a shortage of 'parts'. The most common statement we heard was "just give us the bits and we'll build you the engine".

We set up a trial and all seemed to be going smoothly at the outset - all the necessary launches happened on time and up to about 7 days in we were still on plan. Then disaster struck! There was a 6 day delay waiting for some key components for the high-pressure compressor due to quality issues at the suppliers. We also suffered a further delay at the testing stage once the engine had finally been built. The natural reaction would normally have been one of disappointment having failed to achieve the 27 day target we had set. However, Ian was quick to use the "self-starter" technique to turn the situation around and encouraged the team that the engine's lead-time of 34 days had actually been an improvement on the initial trial engine, and indeed was **the shortest lead-time achieved to date by any engine.** There was success, albeit not to the extent that we had hoped. We were travelling in the right direction, we just needed to keep travelling for a bit longer.

It was now October 2003. The year-end was almost only an engine lead-time away. We had to move fast to achieve the "inevitable dream". I had received great encouragement from the way in which the production leadership team was now starting to embrace the challenge - the "inevitable dream" - and both Ian and I had started to **believe without doubt** that we could build in less than 27 days and more importantly, we really believed that 20 days was possible.

I arranged a meeting to review the data from the second trial, inviting all the production leaders and shop controllers from the build areas. I shared with them my belief that we could improve on the 27 day plan and that we could actually deliver the plan - the "inevitable dream".

To this day I am still amused when I recall what ensued in the meeting for the next half an hour. It looked like a scene from a junior school art lesson as scissors and sellotape were used to great effect to produce a collage-like plan for a 20 day engine. There was so much experience in that room. Everything you needed to know about building an engine and also how we could do things differently to improve the likelihood of success. People talk about reaching a "flow" state; I think we all experienced it that day. More importantly, we all shared the "inevitable dream".

So we had a plan for the 20 day engine.

For our 3rd trial, we wanted to delay the launch of the trail engine as late as possible to give more time for all of the parts to arrive into the stores for kitting. The business was still suffering from contract problems with deliveries to the customer and that led to some unwanted pressure from the Customer Project department to launch earlier than we wanted to. Clearly, not everyone shared our belief.

For the 3 weeks leading up to the launch date we went into super-planning mode. Each production leader produced a detailed milestone plan for his area. We visited suppliers - particularly those with a history of delivery issues - and explained what we were trying to do and the importance of their contribution. When the parts arrived, the storekeepers pre-kitted and quality checked them ready for launch. On Friday 14th November, we held the final planning review. The engine was set for launch the following Monday, 17th November. Every key stakeholder had a committed plan of action. Collectively we were ready to deliver the "inevitable dream".

As with the previous trial, all went well in the first few days. We had decided to share the progress of the project via the Company intranet and I spent the these first few days wandering around the various build areas photographing team members who were working on the engine and posting them with the latest news for the wider consumption. It was around day 5 that I received the first surprise. The assembly management team were forecasting that all of the modules would be completed by the end of the weekend - a staggering 4 days earlier than we had planned for. This put us ahead of the plan for the time being and gave us some breathing space should we encounter any problems later in the assembly process. There was 9 further days of assembly planned before the engine was due to be put onto the test bed which included building the modules into the core stack, dressing the fan case and then attaching the two parts together. It sounds easy but believe me, it's engineering fitting at its most skilled and includes the attachment, by hand, of thousands of components.

And then for the second surprise. On the morning of Wednesday 26th November I arrived at work to discover that the engine core and the fan case had been successfully "married" and tipped during the night shift. We were now 5 days ahead of the plan. Just the core dressing and fitting of the fan and the engine would be ready for test. At this rate we stood the chance of achieving 15 days and you could sense the **desire and belief** in the production team that it was there for the taking.

There were no problems encountered during the remaining assembly activities and the engine went to test on Friday 28th November, commencing its test cycle at 10.30am.

Having successfully completed the testing cycle late on Friday evening, it was now down to the despatch team to complete the final preparations before the engine could be declared complete. Working through the weekend, the team did a great job and by mid-afternoon on Sunday 30th November we had achieved something that most people had considered an "impossible goal" only a few months earlier. We had bettered our 20 day goal and delivered a 14 day engine. Not quite the 10 day engine that had been the aspirational dream back in 2000, but something that proved just what is possible – or "inevitable" - when you harness the power of focus, inspiration, resilience and enthusiasm - in this case, of the work-force.

The use of the tools and techniques from Mike Finnigan's training course had now started to take wider root within the organisation – indeed by mid-2004, more individuals had been through the "impossible to inevitable" experience.

And so, we had turned our "impossible goal" into an "inevitable dream" of winning the Chief Executive's Quality Award, one of the highest awards in Rolls Royce, and in 2005 we did just that.

Thanks Trevor, and Mike, for showing us the way!

Tony Burns joined i2i New Zealand in September 2009.

RELATE AND ASSIMILATE

So, Trevor and Tony's vision took an engine from 400 days to 14, showing the company a glimpse of the future, removing limiting beliefs and leading to potential savings of hundreds of millions of pounds.

It just goes to show what can be done with inspirational leadership. These guys reminded me that when we dream we need to dream big; that we need to inspire those around us with our dreams; and that anything really is possible.

What did they teach you?

1

2

3

'SOMEWHERE OVER THE RAINBOW'

Mike's Introduction

Well, this has to be my favourite, but only for the obvious reason. Whenever I tell Pauline's story on the course, it draws gasps of astonishment, and no wonder. When you read it you'll see why. She uses some technical terms, and mentions her new husband, Dad to me and my wife Cheryl, and Grandad to Lucy, Rose, Grace and Daisy.

First, you're going to read what Polly (Pauline) wrote in her own words, which starts with the break up of her first marriage, after over 30 years, then it's the interview; she just had to be different!

The problem though, is that ever since one of our clients, the Davenham Group, demanded a personal appearance, Pauline is more in demand than I am, and that's not funny. What a story, enjoy!

The Story

'Hello, I'm Polly; I'm a PPL(H), a Helicopter Pilot.

Sounds wonderful, doesn't it? A woman flying helicopters, must be a very privileged person or be wealthy. Read on.

In 1993, the most precious things in my life were my family, my home and my business. One day I was happy, the next, 23rd December, I stood to lose it all.

A very wonderful man called Mike Finnigan took the trouble to advise me; he looked at the situation, he wrote a plan, which, with a lot of hard work on my part, could succeed. From a hopeless situation, there was a chance.

Over the next few years, I stuck to the plan. I literally lived on BEANS, homemade soup, and the odd packet of cigarettes. I never went out socialising; I really didn't have the money. My friends were fantastic, and my family, without them I wouldn't have survived. One of my sisters used to call me and say, 'could you manage a boiled egg and a brandy for your tea love?' Yes I could! Luxury!

Mike came to see me and knew by my enthusiasm I had got through the worst. Had he not taken those hours to talk to me, to make the plan, I would never have made it.

At this stage, I never again, after that experience, allowed myself lingering negative thoughts. I learned that positive thinking works. Before Mike left me that day, I said to him, 'I'm on the up, I'm going to learn to fly and I'm going to have a Rolls Royce too'.

He laughed and kissed me and said to let him know when I did it, I'd be his top achiever!

I won't explain just yet how I did it, but what comes next is almost UNBELIEVABLE, but true just the same.

My best friend in the entire world (David Wood) took me supposedly to Southport, but we never got there. We arrived at Blackpool instead. I did not even say, 'this is not the way', it was just great to be free for a few hours.

Blackpool, believe it or not, was Blackpool Airport. My friend had some business there, he said, well it was MONKEY BUSINESS!

A rather smart chap in flying gear approached me and asked would I like to go out in a helicopter, whilst my friend was talking to the boss. I couldn't believe what I heard, but agreed, and the wonderful man took me chasing birds on the beach, flying high over Blackpool Tower, sweeping down again to watch the Sandpipers. It was like being in a James Bond film! I pinched myself, because compared with tins of beans, this was living!

Walking back to the Heli-centre, the pilot said he'd been told I would like to fly, and asked if I would like to learn to fly a helicopter. I told him my education was very basic, that I ran my own business, which was now successful, and that even if I could afford it, which I could not, I wasn't sure of my ability. Then I corrected myself, I told him that if I could afford it I would do it, but the money was the problem. Positive thinking! He then asked, was I game if the money was available? My answer was yes, and then the fun began.

I was sponsored to fly. I will explain later.

My first lesson was Friday; I had to be on time, wearing sturdy shoes and trousers.

Now a helicopter is probably a million times more difficult to fly than a fixed wing aircraft, and the first lesson is to keep it straight and level. Easy said! Weeks later, I was straight and level.

Then they threw the books at me. Air Law, Meteorology, Navigation, Technical Data, to name but a few; I couldn't even carry the books, let alone learn what was in them!

I set myself a task. Every night, without fail, when I arrived home after a ten hour day, I studied. It took me two years, the learning is awesome, but I sat every exam and EVENTUALLY, I passed. **So much for a lack of education, what's all that in the path of positive thinking!** No chance!

Now I had to learn to hover.

My instructor said, 'Polly, this is a big field. Keep this aircraft in this field and I will be proud of you.' It wasn't big enough at first! Then he just kept finding smaller and smaller fields until we had cracked it, I HOVERED! It took a long time, but I did it.

Next comes THE SOLO, where the student goes alone. **I am five feet tall, weigh seven stones, and am too light to fly a helicopter. I have to fly with a 17Kg bag of bricks so I can get down from the sky.** I fly high like a bird, but then the bird deserts me and I can't land, so with my bag of bricks I can return to tell the tale.

THE SOLO, the most awesome task I have ever faced in my life!

My instructor told me I'd done well at the end of one lesson, then said, 'if I got out now, put your bricks in, and left you ALONE, how would you feel?' I wanted to say I would be back home in two minutes and he would never see me again! I calmly said, 'Fine, yes, fine.' I think it was me.

So that was it then, I had to go or look like a complete idiot. I took off. The sweat was running into my eyes, I was stuck to the seat and my clothes were soaked, but I WAS FLYING, ALL BY MYSELF! My feet didn't touch the ground for days! Of course, I could hardly tell anyone about it, I mean, who would have believed me anyway?

Obi Wan and Luke would have been proud of me!

There was worse to come though. In a helicopter, the right hand steers, the left pulls the power, your feet are on the pedals, and the headset and microphone almost totally cover your face, especially a little one like mine!

Now, I am totally left handed, so I really didn't know what the right was doing!

'Polly, time for a 'Land Away'.

'A what, Bob?'

'If I say this quickly, it won't sound so bad. You have to fly into Liverpool Airport, land, then return here.'

'Me? Alone? Which way is Liverpool?' I'm only six and a half stone by now!

Bob just laughed.

Whilst your hands, feet and face are fully occupied, you also have to operate the radio on different frequencies for different airspace! Liverpool meant speaking to Blackpool, Woodvale, Liverpool Approach, and Liverpool Tower, and my radio would only hold two frequencies, so I had to fly and keep changing it! The aircraft nosedived several times, but I got there.

I'm nudging six stones now, and here comes Bob again. 'I think you're ready for the flight test Polly'. 'Am I, Bob?' 'Yes, nothing to it. All you have to do is take out a CAA Examiner, fly him around a bit, show him what you can do, and if you do okay, you should pass.'

'Oh, is that all Bob?'

'Yes Polly, that's all'.

On the day, I arrived at the airfield at 10.30 am and was still there at 5 pm. As I went in, a rather formidable looking gentleman said, 'are you Polly?' 'Oh no I thought, that's him, look at him!'

He gave me the keys to HIS helicopter. I'd never seen it before in my life. He told me to fire it up; he'd be along in a minute. He was very experienced, told me where he wanted me to go and what he expected.

I thought, 'if he asks me for an AUTOROTATION or a SLOPING LANDING, I'll probably give him a heart attack too, and me! An autorotation means cutting the engine at altitude and landing safely. Piece of cake, eh? I'm 58 by this time, 14th August 1999! And not even six stone! (Joking)

When we got back, he didn't say a word. He just asked me to close the machine down, and he left me there. I walked back to the centre, not a word. Two hours later he came to see me. 'Congratulations, Polly, you're a Pilot!'

Before I finish, let me say that three incredible things have given me a lust for life:

Firstly, my beautiful daughter-in-law, Cheryl, and my grand-daughters, Lucy, Rose, Grace and Daisy.

Secondly, a young man who, from the moment I set eyes on him, I loved him, I am very proud to say I am Pauline Finnigan Wood, and Michael Finnigan is my son.

Finally, my best friend in all the world, my flying sponsor, who is now my husband, the exhilarating, exciting David Wood, my James Bond.

Every moment we spend together is *Over The Rainbow*.

My peers and I are now pensioners. Recently, my life long girl friend, 'DoDo', said to me, 'Are you happy Polly?', 'I am DoDo,' I said. 'Good,' she said, 'We're on the last bus kid!'

David and I bought the R22 we had learned in when we retired. If you are going to dream, you might as well dream big!

Be positive!

L o v e
Polly

The Interview

Mike   *Pauline, people will have read this story about the R22 and you flying and all that kind of stuff but I'm going to take you back to December 1993 to when all this started - you were 52 years old and the start of reality, as you said in that story, was you couldn't buy food, yet you faced me with that conversation where you said 'I want to fly a helicopter' and although I might have never said anything, I was thinking, 'you're mad! You can't even buy food! How the hell are you going to fly a helicopter! How the hell are you going to drive a Rolls Royce one day!' that was what I was thinking.*

        So what was the goal, what was your perspective on it?

Polly   The first part of the goal was to succeed with the plan that you had talked me into putting into action, which was tremendously important. Stop having negative thoughts, be positive - get on with it; which I did.

        But the more wonderful thing to come out of that was making myself realise that negative thoughts were totally useless.

Mike   *So why was that so powerful for you then?*

Polly   It was powerful because at that time I was in a position where I might have lost a property that was worth somewhere between £150,000 and £170,000, also a business property that was worth £70,000 plus a business and I had very little money.

Mike   *How much were you living off then? Come on I remember, I'm checking out whether you remember?*

Polly   £8 a week.

Mike   *And what did you have to buy out of that?*

Polly   I had to buy a tin of beans.

Mike   *So, food?*

Polly   Yes I had to pay for other normal things too. I would say personal spending was between £8 and £10 and I never in all that time, spent more.

Mike   *And you lived like that for two years?*

Polly   I didn't let myself spend over, not once - because the most precious thing I wanted to keep hold of was the home, because it was for my family and my granddaughters. It was bad enough them having no granddad, but it would have been worse if they couldn't have come to my home, their home.

Mike	And I don't think anyone else would have understood that - you fought for that very hard.
Polly	Yes, after badgering the poor building society manager - I would be sat on his bench in his building society and I could see his face wincing, thinking 'oh no, that bloody woman - what does she want?' He would say 'I'd jump through hoops for you to lend you the money if I could,' and in the end one day he put his hands up and said 'OK you win'.
Mike	How many times did you go in?
Polly	Twelve.
Mike	Twelve times to get a mortgage?
Polly	Yes, so that eventually he would call the boss Mr Bullock and sort it out. I'd take a bunch of flowers, tell him I'd paid up on other loans, you know what I mean, it wasn't as if I wanted the money for taking holidays! I mean I knew you were taking on responsibilities, but I realised after two months I'd paid every penny and was keeping up with it!
Mike	And if you can do it for two months, you can do it three - and if you can do it for three, you can do it for four - and you end up doing it for two years or more?
Polly	And THEN you end up saying I want a Rolls Royce, because if I can get through what I got through, I can fly, and I said this repeatedly, and I never knew about positive thinking, I'd had a very limited education.
Mike	I suppose at that time if I'm honest as well I would be looking at you thinking 'you're mad - you can't even buy food, you're not even eating!'
Polly	That was true because I can remember one conversation about going to the doctors and having to go back, because I was underweight. He said I had to come and be checked. I had seen the nurse a few weeks previously and they weren't happy.
Mike	And you had your back problem too.
Polly	Carrying things upstairs I literally ruptured a disc, but anyway I had an 'iron jacket' for about 18 months!
Mike	Yes you did, you wore it all the time.
Polly	I even went to bed in it. We called it a tin vest!
Mike	So you've got a 52 year old woman in a tin vest on £8 a week talking about driving a Rolls Royce and flying a helicopter! Mad! I thought I was the dreamer. That's my job, remember!

Polly	But exactly! Let me remind you, you put me on the path; had you not, and this is tremendously important, had you not set me on that path, I could have lost a home and a business property. You set the path for me, so therefore my ultimate aim became when I started to think seriously about flying - 'I'll fly Michael!'
Mike	*Well we'll talk about that for a minute because that is brilliant.*
Polly	'I'll fly Michael', but then when I used to go on the furrows; one furrow I went on one day was leaving Blackpool going to Woodvale, finding Standish coming back up the M6 to the M55 turning in, coming in via the gas holders at Blackpool, at the airport, and all the time I flew that journey I was absolutely terrified, I was on my own, but I was pretending to fly you in my mind!
Mike	*I'm sitting next to you am I?*
Polly	In my mind you're with me - absolutely! Every inch! I got through it all, and David and my teacher showed so much enthusiasm and never once despite all that was happening did they say, 'are you scared?', 'are you apprehensive?', 'are you uncomfortable?' - nothing, there were never negative discussions. We were all probably terrified, but there were never negative discussions, and I don't think I ever once said to David, 'I don't want to do this', even if it was terrifying.
Mike	*And you need cushions behind you, I know.*
Polly	Yes, five inches of cushion to push me forward, because my legs are five inches too short.
Mike	*And you're 40lbs too light, so you don't reach the minimum safe weight for flying, so have to carry a little parcel with you as well! So, apart from not having the money, and never having done it before, and never having even flown in a helicopter before, you're too old, and too small - what were you thinking about?*
Polly	If you've sat and watched any bird - a bird always takes off into, or it lifts up and turns up into, wind - it gets transitional lift, everything that's flying gets transitional lift, but once the helicopter has got the transitional lift, it can hover, and it's magical.
Mike	*How long have you thought like that, is that something that occurred to you as a little girl?*

Polly	I remember talking with your granddad – he used to have a book with an aeroplane in that was a pop-up type – it wasn't in a pop-up book, it was in an encyclopaedia of technology – I think I've still got it. It all opened up and your granddad used to talk to me about it when I was little.
	Sometimes we would look at that book four times a week... maybe more, and he would say, 'you will live in a time when everyone, even you will fly.' It was in 1948, something like that, so really that is where the flying love came from.
Mike	*So all that time, all through those dark days, 1994/95 really, we used to talk about driving a Rolls Royce – flying a helicopter – how many times did you think about that?*
Polly	Many, many times!
Mike	*You always said it to me, always!*
Polly	Even I stop and pinch myself – that my life is so wonderful.
	I have stopped and pinched myself and made myself realise that it is real – that it is happening, after being to the bottom of the pit, and coming out of the pit, and you go to the other end of the spectrum where it is as good as it gets!
Mike	*But I think that what is impressive about your story, I tell it all the time, is that it is unbelievable! That is why it is so important for me to get this down; I think people almost can't get their heads round it!*
Polly	And it is really hard to fly a helicopter. It is probably the achievement I am most proud of – my pilot's licence.
Mike	*I'm sure it is. As a conclusion this is your chance to send a message to other people who are embarking on their journey.*
Polly	The most important thing you have to do is believe in yourself, and think positive, and when a negative thought comes, you've got to stop yourself, and push it out of the way!
	If you say, 'I feel lousy today' then you will feel lousy. If you say, 'I feel good today, I'm going to achieve today', it changes the spectrum completely.

The future belongs to those who believe in the beauty of their dreams

Eleanor Roosevelt

RELATE AND ASSIMILATE

*This is my **Mum**! She truly is an amazing person. She taught me that people can do anything they put their minds to. All through her hard times, she never lost sight of her dreams. She took the time to develop huge goals, audacious dreams, and kept them not where most people leave them, at the back of their minds, but at the very front of her mind, for almost every waking moment, and held onto them no matter what life threw at her.*

Please, please do the same, because all things are possible to those who just keep believing.

Thanks Mum, for this most valuable of all lessons, and for always being there for me and encouraging me, your daughter-in-law Cheryl, and your granddaughters to chase their own dreams.

What did Pauline teach you?

1

2

3

THE LAST WORD

By

Michael Finnigan

I hope you enjoyed that. So many people, my family, my colleagues, my customers and my friends have inspired me to choose a career path which I feel privileged to have found.

They all know who they are, and how much I love, respect and admire them. Andrew O'Donoghue and Tom Young deserve special mentions for their tireless work re-crafting and re-editing this book. Andrew and I have known each other and worked together for a long time, and his personal friendship and professional guidance are priceless.

This book has taken so long to conceive and produce, and my journey so far has been a challenging and rewarding one.

There are already developments to the stories told in these pages, and many new stories of success, achievement and outrageous victories against all the odds.

As I write, I am gathering new material, covering successes for people in relationships, business, sport, health, and charitable endeavours, each one inspiring and uplifting. As our new businesses spring into life around the globe, we will bolster the existing international dimension of our stories.

Thank you for reading along with us, for sharing the passion, and remember; we are waiting to help you turn seemingly

'impossible' challenges into 'inevitable' dreams

Michael Finnigan

You can contact me at michael@i2i-121.com or visit the company's website for further information. www.i2i-121.com

WHAT THE CORPORATES SAY

An up to date list of i2i clients can be found on the web at www.i2i-121.com; here are a few sound bites to be going on with

Michael Finnigan is an inspirational, motivational and often thought provoking self help expert.

His company, i2i, has the ability to give people the knowledge to raise their own bars, expectations and ultimately performance both in their personal and professional lives.

Their enthusiasm, empathy and in depth understanding of what really drives our behaviours is delivered in a way that is very easy to understand and apply.

In 2009, i2i delivered a programme for our sales team which helped grow our new business sales by £5 million per week, almost a 500% increase, making it without question the best programme we ever ran - ever.

Head of Sales Development, Royal Mail

'i2i recently worked with over 120 people managers within A&L Commercial Bank, from Directors to team leaders.

The key message Michael and the team were to share was Positively Leading and Communicating 'Change'.

As A&L had recently been taken over by Santander, it was crucial this programme was successful and that the content shared experiences and gave valuable tools in being able to deal with the mental challenges of positive leadership during change.

Not only was the programme a success, but Michael was also a real role model. It really helped put some perspective on a challenging time within A&L.'

Head of Learning, Santander

'I refer to Mike Finnigan as 'Mr Motivator'. That's because every time he addresses an audience, people float out of the room feeling so much better than when they walked in.   He encourages people to be positive and have self-belief; critical skills required when starting and growing a business.   If only it were possible, I'd bottle up 'Mr Motivator' and offer a daily dose to all business owners! '

Emma Jones, Founder of Enterprise Nation [www.enterprisenation.com] the home business website, and author of 'Spare Room Start Up – how to start a business from home'

I'd say Mike has been one of the most influential people that I have ever come across.   Being around him is the equivalent of a two week holiday. His energy and positivity is infectious; his behavioural insights astounding.

He talks the talk and walks that walk consistently.

I've been lucky enough to meet a few great people in my career - but Mike, you're in another league - you truly are remarkable!

Head of Corporate Affairs, Royal Liver

ABOUT THE AUTHOR

Michael has been working with individuals, teams and businesses all over the world since 1992. His clients include the world's largest organisations and some of the most adored and recognised people too.

Inspired by the lives and teachings of two great men, W Clement Stone and Art Niemann, Michael agreed to take their message to the next generation and his team now extends to New York, Cape Town and Christchurch, New Zealand, a global force for change soon to include the Arab world too.

Michael's work shows people and businesses how to face up to seemingly 'impossible' challenges and turn them into 'inevitable' successes. Michael has taught all over the world and considers himself privileged to have either met or worked with (or against!), the Dalai Lama, Ron Dennis, Frank Carson, Sir Alex Ferguson, Jose Mourinho, Sam Allardyce, Darren Clarke, Dame Mary Peters, Tiger Woods, David Moyes, Bill Kenwright, Andrew Flintoff, Duncan Fletcher, Wayne Rooney, Martin Johnson, Last Titanic Survivor Milvina Dean, Everest Climber Annabelle Bond, Dancing On Ice's Karen Barber, Adrian Childs, Jimmy Carr, Derek Hatton, Gary Player, Sir Derek Higgs, Nelson Mandela, Pioneering Artists 'Temper' and Willard Wiggan, Archbishop Desmond Tutu, Phillip Schofield, Dr Patch Adams, Saatchi's Kevin Roberts, Jimmy White, Pelé, Will Carling, Sir Tom Finney, Shane Warne, Billionaire Phillip Green, Sylvester Stallone, Colin Montgomery, Arsène Wenger, Gerry Adams, Stephen Hendry, Sir Matthew Pinsent, Hayley Mills, Beth Tweddle, Polar Explorer Torry Laursen, Sir Clive Woodward, Fred Reichheld, William Hague, Gordon Banks, the original Horse Whisperer Monty Roberts, world renowned Cancer Specialist Dr Rosy Daniels, and even John Motson, Cristiano Ronaldo, and the Australian Cricket Team.

Lightning Source UK Ltd.
Milton Keynes UK
15 November 2010

162905UK00002B/2/P

9 781449 044268